PUBLIC MANAGEMENT DEVELOPMENTS

UPDATE 1994

ORGANISATION FOR ECONOMIC CO-OPERATION AND DEVELOPMENT

ORGANISATION FOR ECONOMIC CO-OPERATION AND DEVELOPMENT

Pursuant to Article 1 of the Convention signed in Paris on 14th December 1960, and which came into force on 30th September 1961, the Organisation for Economic Co-operation and Development (OECD) shall promote policies designed:

— to achieve the highest sustainable economic growth and employment and a rising standard of living in Member countries, while maintaining financial stability, and thus to contribute to the development of the world economy;

— to contribute to sound economic expansion in Member as well as non-member countries in the process of economic development; and

— to contribute to the expansion of world trade on a multilateral, non-discriminatory basis in accordance with international obligations.

The original Member countries of the OECD are Austria, Belgium, Canada, Denmark, France, Germany, Greece, Iceland, Ireland, Italy, Luxembourg, the Netherlands, Norway, Portugal, Spain, Sweden, Switzerland, Turkey, the United Kingdom and the United States. The following countries became Members subsequently through accession at the dates indicated hereafter: Japan (28th April 1964), Finland (28th January 1969), Australia (7th June 1971), New Zealand (29th May 1973) and Mexico (18th May 1994). The Commission of the European Communities takes part in the work of the OECD (Article 13 of the OECD Convention).

Publié en français sous le titre :
ÉVOLUTIONS DANS LA GESTION PUBLIQUE :
MISE A JOUR 1994

FOREWORD

This report updates the Public Management Committee's publication *Public Management Developments: Survey 1993* (OECD, Paris, 1993). It summarises initiatives in public sector management reform taken during 1993 as reported by OECD countries and has been compiled in close collaboration with a network of national correspondents designated for this purpose.

The report consists of three parts: an overview of trends prepared by David Rushforth of the OECD Secretariat on the basis of the contributions received; country chapters on developments in 1993 provided by national correspondents; and a statistical annex prepared by Bernard Feys of the Secretariat from country inputs.

At its meeting on 7-8 April 1994, the Public Management Committee agreed to recommend that the report be made available to the public on the responsibility of the Secretary-General of the OECD.

TABLE OF CONTENTS

OVERVIEW

Information received from OECD countries for this report suggests that there has been a reinforcement of the main trends in public sector management reform as identified in the previous publication in this series, *Public Management Developments: Survey 1993*. In that publication, reform trends were grouped, for illustrative purposes, into two broad sets as follows:

- attempts to adjust the size and structure of the public sector by seeking to make it leaner, more competitive, less centralised and able to provide more choice; and
- efforts to improve public sector management by enhancing the effectiveness of, in particular, the financial, personnel, performance and regulatory management functions.

Country reporting is also consistent with the conclusions of the recent report to the Public Management Committee, ''Governance in Transition'' planned for publication later this year. That report points in particular to the fact that traditional governance structures and managerial responses are ineffectual in today's context of major structural change, and aims to outline the main strategies adopted to remedy this situation.

The following comments indicate the broad nature and direction of public sector management reform activities across OECD countries in 1993. They seek to illustrate, in a selective manner, the more innovative changes and to give a flavour of the variety of initiatives being taken. They cannot, of course, fully cover the many measures reported in detail in the individual country chapters.

The results of the enquiry show that there have been important efforts to adjust the size and structure of the public sector. Privatisation is continuing in many countries and some, for example Turkey, report plans to accelerate the process. The drive towards more widespread use of market-type mechanisms is also being maintained. Numerous significant steps have also been taken in countries to further commercialise and/or corporatise public bodies. In other fields of public management reform, efforts to improve the management of policy-making and regulatory reforms have continued, as for example in Switzerland where more flexibility and less regulation are the core of current reforms at the centre of government. Canada and a number of other countries have also noted advances in the management of information technology, but it is in the areas of performance management, the management of financial and human resources, and improving relations with citizens/enterprises that most change is reported.

Recognition of the need for public sector management reform is also growing, as, for example, illustrated by the National Performance Review in the United States. This major initiative led by the Vice-President reviewed the operations of the federal government with the aim of restructuring and streamlining to create a government that ''works better and costs less''.

Limits to size and spending

It is in this area of centrally-imposed constraints on public sector pay and recruitment that most new reform measures were reported in the 1993 enquiry. This tendency might be seen as inconsistent with, if not contradictory to, the trend to more devolved management and less centralised government. In Canada salaries of public servants were frozen for two years and operating costs for all departments were reduced by 3 per cent for the next two fiscal years, and in Greece the freeze on appointments and recruitment has continued. There will be a freeze on running costs in 1994/95 in the United Kingdom; departments will be expected to keep pay budgets (which represent 60 per cent of total running costs) to the 1993/94 level, and to finance any increases in pay in 1994/95 from improvements in productivity. In the United States, the administration is requiring agencies to reduce employment by 12 per cent over the next five years, while the Budget Enforcement Act set spending caps to fiscal year 1997 that place a ceiling on federal spending. In Luxembourg, the Commission on Economy and Rationalisation submits monthly reports to the Prime Minister suggesting which vacant posts should not be filled, with the aim of re-attributing only two-thirds of those vacant.

Decentralisation and deconcentration

Decentralisation to sub-national government and deconcentration within central government, if taken together, represent the most significant structural change reported by Member countries during 1993. In France, for example, administrative deconcentration was the main thrust of reform in 1993. The Interministerial Committee for Territorial Administration there decided to produce guidelines for the re-organisation and deconcentration of each ministry. In Sweden, a new system of government grants to local authorities was introduced and numerous earmarked grants were discontinued. In the United Kingdom, 16 new agencies were launched as part of the "Next Steps" initiative.

The redistribution of roles and responsibilities between central, regional and local levels of government has also been significant in numerous countries. In Austria, debate focused on the federal and *Land* levels in the context of entry to the European Union; while in Japan, the Prime Minister designated the first 15 pilot communities as part of the "Special Scheme for Promoting Decentralisation". In Finland, new "Guidelines for Reforming the Central and Regional Administration" aim at structural changes and a redefinition of the roles of each level of government; while in the Netherlands, negotiations on conditions of employment have been decentralised such that the Ministry of Home Affairs is now only the employer of central government staff and not those in, for example, provinces or municipalities. In Spain, important progress has been made in better distributing State taxes amongst the Autonomous Communities, whose share in total public expenditure has increased from 6.1 per cent in 1982 to 24.3 per cent in 1993.

Improving relations with citizens and enterprises

There has been much evidence of continuing efforts to improve the administration's relations with both citizens and enterprises. This was manifest in two principal domains: the further development of citizens' charters (for example in Belgium, France, Portugal and the United Kingdom) and in the setting up of various forms of one-stop shops (for example, in Norway, Portugal and Sweden).

Performance management

Countries are developing performance indicators and targets more extensively across the public sector and they are being made more public. Thus, in Denmark, a new concept of "service standard statements" is being developed by the Ministry of Finance for organisation-specific application across the public sector; and in Finland, the Ministry of Finance has set up a "Quality and Productivity Project" with several sectoral pilot projects and guidelines on quality management and cost control methods. The "Government Performance and Results Act" was enacted in the United States. It requires agencies to develop strategic plans and prepare annual performance goal plans by 1997, and to report actual performance against goals by 1999. Pilot agencies are being selected for tests over the next three years.

Financial resources management

The two main tendencies in financial resource management continue to be to provide, often at the same time, more rigorous accounting methods to strengthen reporting on results, and greater flexibility through more recourse to frameworks in forms such as multi-year budgeting and the specification of general guidelines rather than detailed requirements. Thus, Australia's Department of Finance is co-ordinating a pilot accrual accounting reporting programme involving 34 public bodies; Belgium has strengthened its use of multi-year budgeting as a management tool; and in Finland, the Budget Decree has been completely rewritten to include instructions on ministerial management of agencies by results.

Human resources management

Numerous steps have been taken in the field of industrial relations. In Australia, a beginning has been reported with the application in agencies of the Workplace Bargaining Agreement between the Government and public sector unions. In France, agreement was reached with five civil service unions to preserve purchasing power in real terms, and on provisions for faster recruitment procedures and proposals for part-time work. Italy has introduced measures to put public sector employment on a more competitive footing with the private sector and with European counterparts. In the Netherlands, the privatisation of the civil servants superannuation fund was agreed between the Minister for Home Affairs and the unions, in principle as of 1 January 1996. And Spain reached an important Administration-Unions Agreement aimed at improving working conditions, including more flexibility and greater decentralisation of responsibilities from central to sectoral bodies.

Regulatory management and reform

Progress has continued with many existing regulatory improvement programmes and several new bodies have been set up to vet new measures. In Iceland, for example, the Prime Minister appointed a Commission on Regulatory Reform to recommend how to lighten regulatory burdens by streamlining regulatory agencies and their activities. In Ireland, a Task Force has been set up by the Minister for Enterprise and Employment to draw up a charter for small business. In Japan, deregulation is seen as a key measure to break out of recession and to promote administrative reform; the interim report of the Advisory Group for Economic Structural Reform put its focus on deregulation. Norway's Ministry of Government Administration prepared a draft checklist for assessing new regulations; and in the United Kingdom, seven task forces of business people set up to conduct an independent review of regulation produced a total of 605 proposals for reform. Principles for good regulation have been defined and will be applied to new regulations by a new Deregulation Task Force. In the United States, all agencies have been directed to conduct a review of regulations, to eliminate one half of executive branch internal regulations and to make the regulatory review process more public.

Evaluation of reforms

It was observed in the 1993 Survey publication that evaluation of reform efforts are largely *ad hoc* and inadequately systematic in most countries. This disappointing situation is tending to prevail despite notable exceptions such as those which follow. In Australia, the report of the independent Task Force on Management Improvement, *The Australian Public Service Reformed: An Evaluation of a Decade of Management Reform*, was the subject of a special presentation by the Prime Minister. Its general conclusions included that the direction of reform was correct, that the benefits far outweigh the costs, but also that they may be more fully integrated into the culture of the public service as a whole. In Austria, the Administrative Management Project was evaluated; and in Finland, the Ministry of Finance's report, *International Comparison Project*, proposed that an evaluation be undertaken of public sector reform policy since 1986.

Efforts at evaluation of reform must be intensified if benefit is to be drawn from experience already gained. This essential management tool should involve both monitoring of how existing reforms need to be corrected and scanning ahead to provide pertinent follow-up steps. Such efforts are especially necessary as many reforms enter new territory where risk-taking has to be calculated and some mistakes are inevitable.

Rating exercise

The two tables and two charts which follow give a general indication of the relative importance of different types of new reform initiatives in 1993 and their distribution across Member countries. The scores have been attributed by each country and are based on the following rating scheme: 2 = "major initiative"; 1 = "less important measure"; 0 = "no significant steps taken". The scores given by each country to some extent reflect the amount of reform activity in each country, but respondents differ in their view of what is a "significant" initiative. This in part reflects the stage in the reform process they have reached and may explain lower scores, for example in Japan, where there has been sustained reform effort since 1981 when the Provisional Commission for Administrative Reform was set up; and in New Zealand which, after major reforms, is now in the process of consolidating them. It also underlines the fact that these are only rough indicators which must be interpreted with due care.

It is clear that there has been an acceleration in reform efforts in many countries, as a result of greater political awareness of the need for change in the public sector, and a considerable globalisation of many governance issues. What needs to be avoided, however, is the impression that febrile reform activity is the norm. The developments reported in this update must be recognised as being part of a process – and their continuity across political change or even between design and implementation will be subject to many influences. Nevertheless, important advances are being made in a number of countries and the efficiency and effectiveness of the public sector are increasingly seen as determining factors in the competitive position of all countries in the international market place.

Table 1.A. **New public sector management initiatives: OECD countries, 1993[1]**

(size and structure of the public sector)

	"Limits to size"	Privatisation	Commercialisation/ corporatisation	Decentralisation to sub-national government	Deconcentration within central government	Use of market-type mechanisms	New roles for central management bodies	Other restructuring/ "rationalisation"
Australia	2	2	2	2	2	1	1	1
Austria	2	1	1	2	2	0	2	1
Belgium	1	1	0	0	0	1	1	2
Canada	2	1	1	1	1	1	2	2
Denmark	0	1	2	0	0	1	0	1
Finland	2	1	2	1	2	1	1	0
France	2	2	1	0	0	1	2	2
Germany	2	2	0	1	0	0	0	2
Greece	1	1	0	0	1	0	0	0
Iceland	2	2	2	0	1	1	0	2
Ireland	2	0	1	0	2	1	1	0
Italy	2	2	2	1	2	1	1	2
Japan	1	1	0	1	0	0	0	1
Luxembourg	2	0	2	2	0	0	0	0
Netherlands	1	1	1	2	2	0	1	2
New Zealand	0	1	1	0	2	2	0	0
Norway	2	0	1	1	1	0	0	0
Portugal	1	1	1	0	2	1	0	1
Spain	2	0	1	2	0	0	2	1
Sweden	1	2	2	2	0	2	1	1
Switzerland	2	1	0	0	0	0	0	0
Turkey	2	2	1	1	0	1	0	0
United Kingdom	2	2	2	2	2	2	0	0
United States	2	0	0	0.5	0	1	0	2
TOTAL	38	27	26	21.5	22	18	15	23

Note: The numbers are purely indicative, and are shown in order to provide a sense of where reform efforts are being placed. They do not permit comparisons between countries.
1. Ratings have been made by national correspondents where 2 = "major initiative"; 1 = "less important measure"; and 0 = "no significant steps taken".

Table 1.B.   **New public sector management initiatives: OECD countries, 1993**[1]

(other main fields of public management reform)

	Management of policy-making	Performance management	Financial resources management	Personnel management	Regulatory management and reform	Improving relations with citizens/enterprises	Management of information technology	"Other"
Australia	2	2	2	2	2	2	2	0
Austria	0	2	1	2	2	1	2	1
Belgium	2	1	1	1	0	2	0	2
Canada	2	1	1	1	1	1	2	0
Denmark	2	2	2	2	0	2	1	1
Finland	1	1	2	1	0	2	1	0
France	2	2	1	2	1	2	1	1
Germany	1	1	2	2	2	1	0	0
Greece	1	1	2	1	0	0	0	0
Iceland	0	0	2	0	2	1	2	2
Ireland	1	1	2	0	2	2	2	2
Italy	2	1	0	2	2	0	0	1
Japan	0	0	0	1	2	1	0	0
Luxembourg	0	0	1	1	1	1	0	2
Netherlands	2	1	1	2	1	1	1	0
New Zealand	1	2	2	1	0	0	2	1
Norway	1	1	1	1	1	2	1	2
Portugal	1	1	2	1	0	1	1	0
Spain	0	2	1	2	0	0	2	0
Sweden	0	1	2	2	1	1	1	1
Switzerland	1	2	1	1	1	1	2	0
Turkey	1	1	1	2	2	2	0	1
United Kingdom	0	1	1	1	2	2	0	0
United States	1.5	2	1	1.5	2	1	0	1
TOTAL	24.5	29	32	32.5	27	29	23	18

Note: The numbers are purely indicative, and are shown in order to provide a sense of where reform efforts are being placed. They do not permit comparisons between countries.
1.   Ratings have been made by national correspondents where 2 = "major initiative"; 1 = "less important measure"; and 0 = "no significant steps taken".

Diagram 1. **New public sector management initiatives: OECD countries, 1993**

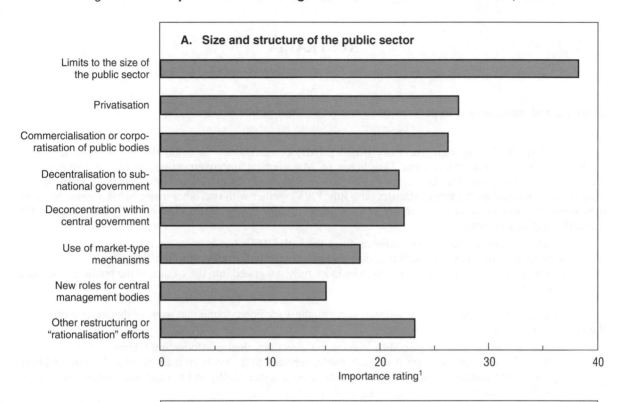

A. Size and structure of the public sector

(Importance rating¹)

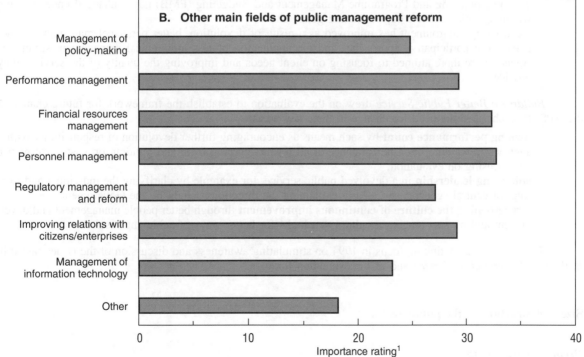

B. Other main fields of public management reform

(Importance rating¹)

1. Aggregation of 24 countries, where for each country, 2 = "major initiative", 1 = "less important measure",
   0 = "no significant steps taken", (see Tables 1.A and 1.B).

AUSTRALIA

Evaluation of management improvement in the Australian public service

In 1991, the Management Advisory Board (MAB) commissioned an evaluation of the past decade of public sector reform. The independent Task Force on Management Improvement completed the evaluation in December 1992. Its report, *The Australian Public Service Reformed: An Evaluation of a Decade of Management Reform*, was launched by the Prime Minister on 1 July 1993 together with two other major MAB papers: *Building a Better Public Service* and *Accountability in the Commonwealth Public Sector*. The general conclusions of the evaluation report were that:

- the direction of management reforms since the early 1980s has been correct;
- these reforms have been well accepted and their benefits far outweigh their costs; but
- there remains room for the reforms to be more fully integrated into the culture of the public service as a whole.

As a result of extensive agency and staff surveys, the Task Force found that some of the positive effects of the reforms were that:

- ministers are now better placed to oversee the directions their portfolios are taking;
- the professional ethos of the Australian public service (APS) has been maintained and reinforced both through the establishment of the Senior Executive Service (SES) and through the overall response of staff to change;
- corporate planning and Programme Management and Budgeting (PMB) have enhanced understanding within agencies of their objectives and goals; and
- the working environment has improved as a result of devolution, better personnel management practices, more participative approaches and the application of less hierarchical management structures. Agencies are more attuned to focusing on client needs and improving the quality of the services they provide.

Building a Better Public Service drew on the evaluation to establish the framework for future change in the APS. It emphasised the need for change in three key areas:

- **making performance count** by such means as encouraging further devolution of responsibility within agencies; rewarding good performance at all levels; learning from and building on past performance and focusing on evaluation;
- **enhancing leadership** in a devolved public service, for example by clarifying the individual and joint roles of central agencies and clearly explaining the directions sought by the Government;
- **strengthening the culture of continuous improvement** through better people management and development and by encouraging a culture that looks for better ways of achieving results.

There will be a continuing focus in 1994 on stimulating awareness and discussion of the issues raised in *Building a Better Public Service* and of the evaluation findings.

Size and structure of the public sector

Organisational change

In March 1993, several Commonwealth departments were renamed following machinery of government changes made after the 13 March general elections. The following departments were renamed:

- the Department of Administrative Services became the Department of the Arts and Administrative Services;
- the Department of the Arts, Sport, the Environment and Territories became the Department of the Environment, Sport and Territories;
- the Department of Health, Housing and Community Services became the Department of Health, Housing, Local Government and Community Services;
- the Department of Immigration, Local Government and Ethnic Affairs became the Department of Immigration and Ethnic Affairs;
- the Department of Industry, Technology and Commerce became the Department of Industry, Technology and Regional Development.

In December 1993, a Department of Communications was created and the Department of Transport and Communications was consequently renamed the Department of Transport. At the same time, the Department of Health, Housing, Local Government and Community Services was renamed the Department of Human Services and Health.

Privatisation

In March 1993, British Airways paid A$665 million for 25 per cent of the Australian Government's equity in Qantas. The Initial Public Offer (IPO) for the remaining 75 per cent equity has been deferred until after the 1993/94 financial year.

In October 1993, the Commonwealth Bank secondary share offer yielded proceeds of A$1.69 billion after taking account of the discount available for retail investors. The remaining equity in the Commonwealth Bank has not fallen below 50.1 per cent.

In November 1993, the sale of the Commonwealth's shares in the Snowy Mountains Engineering Corporation Limited (SMEC) to its staff was completed. This sale is significant in that it is the first staff buy-out of a Commonwealth asset.

Commercialisation

Within the APS, the commercialisation process has been accelerated and broadened in recent years. Charging for services is now widespread among Commonwealth agencies and has been developed in response to a need to improve resource allocation, responsiveness to client needs and accountability. Some agencies are developing further forms of commercialisation, including progressive untying of clients' preparation of business plans, specification of performance targets in terms of returns on assets, and development of dividend policies.

Commercialisation has generally been applied on a case-by-case basis. The Department of Finance is developing general policy principles for commercialisation drawing on best practices that have emerged to date.

Outsourcing/contracting

A MAB/MIAC study, published in December 1992, found no regulatory impediments to contracting in the APS.

Policy on information technology was revised in 1991 to require agencies to test the market for the outsourcing of both new and existing information technology (IT) service requirements. In July 1993, the Department of Finance published *Value for Your IT Dollar* to assist agencies to assess the costs and benefits of current and alternative methods of IT service provision.

In response to an Australian National Audit Office recommendation on outsourcing of the Department of Veterans' Affairs National Computer Centre, the Public Service Commission (PSC) – in consultation with the Departments of Finance and Industrial Relations – is developing a more comprehensive policy framework for dealing with the staffing aspects of outsourcing. Aspects addressed include the extent to which the Commonwealth brokers jobs and conditions with the new employer. Staffing and industrial arrangements associated with the sale of a major Commonwealth repatriation hospital to the private sector were also concluded during 1993.

The Department of the Arts and Administrative Services, which has responsibility for issuing procurement guidelines, is producing a handbook on contracting out.

Government business enterprises (GBEs)

The Minister for Finance announced, on 5 August 1993, a package of measures to enhance the accountability and performance of Commonwealth GBEs. These measures, which build on the earlier reforms, are designed to lead to further improvements in GBE performance, as well as better Government oversight of its GBEs. Some of the main features of the package, which will apply from 1993/94, include:

- an increased focus on ''world best practice'' by GBEs;
- GBE boards to have greater authority and responsibility for performance, and more freedom to manage commercially with a reduction in some controls (*e.g.* industrial relations and superannuation arrangements); and
- clarification and reinforcement of each GBE's commercial objectives and any community service obligations.

Monitoring of GBE performance is also being enhanced by means of a report to Cabinet each year, provided by the Minister for Finance and which assesses the financial performance of all GBEs.

Other main fields of public management reform

Workplace bargaining

1993 saw further advances following on from the achievement of an APS Workplace Bargaining Agreement between the Government and the public sector unions in December 1992 (the APS Agreement). This Agreement provides for an initial APS-wide increase based on productivity improvements, two general economic adjustments (in March of 1993 and 1994), and a framework and principles for the introduction of workplace-level bargaining in APS agencies.

To support the development of innovative agency-level agreements based on workplace reform, the APS Division of the Department of Industrial Relations has been re-organised with a greater client focus by providing training in the new skills required, information-sharing and advice. The strategy to support agencies, in particular small agencies, includes the provision of consultancy service and delivery of a series of conferences and workshops and other activities specially targeted to their needs.

Several agencies are making substantial progress towards achieving an agency agreement, and in principle agreement has been reached in the Department of Defence. Gradual progress to date is not surprising, given the magnitude of the changes involved, the fact that agencies need to cope with a major cultural shift from centralised arrangements to a more decentralised approach, and the complexity of some of the issues which must be resolved through the vehicle of workplace bargaining.

Some of the areas of productivity improvement being considered at the agency level include:

- changes in work organisation, job design and working patterns and arrangements;
- streamlining, rationalising and enhancing the use of technology;
- enhancing the quality and provision of training; and
- the introduction of quality assurance and continuous improvement programmes.

A further initiative included with the APS Agreement has been the introduction of performance-based pay for management levels of the APS.

Performance management

Performance appraisal and pay

Performance appraisal programmes were introduced across the APS in 1991/92 and now cover management levels in more than 90 APS agencies. The system complements the recent initiatives in the APS to enhance agency productivity. Performance pay focuses attention on individual performance of middle and senior managers who play a key role in managing workplace reform, while rewards under agency workplace bargaining will reflect organisational and team performance.

Performance pay is only available subject to officers' eligibility being determined through a rigorous performance appraisal process, including the provision of privacy safeguards and grievance/appeal mechanisms. SES and senior officers who have completed appraisal cycles are able to access performance bonuses, which are at risk and need to be earned annually. Performance appraisal and performance pay processes are complemented by enhanced means to deal with underperforming officers.

Experience elsewhere highlights the need for ongoing review and refinement of these schemes to ensure their most effective operation. Overall review processes have been built into the scheme in agencies and across the APS so the experiences in the initial round can be evaluated.

The PSC has conducted an interim review of the implementation of performance appraisal across the APS and has provided a preliminary report to MAB. A full report on the implementation experience will be completed early in 1994.

The Senate Standing Committee on Finance and Public Administration undertook an inquiry into the implementation of performance pay in the latter half of 1993 and reported to Parliament in December 1993. The Government will respond to this report in 1994.

A full evaluation of the arrangements for performance appraisal and pay will be undertaken by the PSC and the Departments of Finance and Industrial Relations towards the end of 1994 when the programme will have been in place for two full cycles.

Evaluation

Evaluation activity has grown substantially in recent years. The July 1993 discussion paper, *The Use of Evaluation in the 1992-93 Budget*, showed that evaluation is making a major contribution to budget deliberations. For example, in the 1992-93 Budget, it is estimated that 36 per cent of new policy proposals (A$859 million) were influenced by evaluation results. Evaluations have provided programme managers with valuable information about the performance of their programmes and the achievement of desired outcomes. Evaluation findings have thus enabled managers continuously to improve their programmes.

Financial resources management

Financial reporting

The Department of Finance is co-ordinating a pilot accrual accounting reporting programme involving 34 departments. Ten departments propose to produce financial statements on an accrual basis for 1992/93 with the remainder doing so for 1993/94. *Financial Statements Guidelines for Departmental Secretaries (Accrual Reporting)* have been developed by the Department of Finance in consultation with the Australian National Audit Office and departments participating in the pilot programme.

Budget reform

Traditionally, Australian federal budgets have been delivered in August. The Australian Government recently decided that they will be delivered prior to the commencement of each financial year to facilitate planning by the public and private sectors. In 1994, the Budget will be delivered on 10 May, covering as previously the year beginning 1 July. The new arrangements will be accompanied by increased prior consultation of minor parties, and changes in the documentation provided for parliamentary scrutiny.

A parliamentary committee is currently conducting an inquiry into the structure and operation of efficiency dividend arrangements. Currently, the dividend involves an annual return to the budget of 1.25 per cent of running costs from most departments and agencies. The Committee was scheduled to report in March 1994.

Personnel management

Equal employment opportunity (EEO)

The Minister assisting the Prime Minister for Public Service Matters launched the "Equal Employment Opportunity Strategic Plan for the Australian Public Service for the 1990s" in May 1993. The focus of the plan is on integrating EEO principles and measures into all personnel management activities in the APS. It incorporates a number of performance indicators including increasing the numbers of Aboriginal and Torres Strait Islander people to 2 per cent of APS employment by the year 2000 and increasing the proportion of women in the SES to 20 per cent by the same year. It is planned to undertake an initial review of the implementation of the Plan in 1994 and a more thorough evaluation in 1999.

Guidelines on official conduct

The PSC is preparing, in consultation with other agencies, a revised draft of the *Guidelines on Official Conduct for Commonwealth Public Servants* for consideration by MAB. Following further consideration by agencies and public sector unions, MAB plans to release the revised guidelines in 1994.

Reference

Department of Finance (1993), *Australian Public Service Statistical Bulletin 1992-93*, Canberra.

AUSTRIA

Public management reform in Austria in 1993 included significant progress in the Administrative Management Project. This work, which was launched in 1989 on the basis of a decision of the Council of Ministers, is being developed and co-ordinated by the Federal Chancellery. During 1993 – the formal last year of the project – reform work focused on the **implementation of reform measures** in different areas of public administration and, at the end of year, in the **preparation of a general report**, its results and evaluation. Some examples in the main fields of implementation could be summarised as follows:

- In an effort to **reduce overlapping competences,** a law on the clarification of fields of responsibility and a law on the reduction of fields of responsibility were passed by Parliament in spring 1993.
- Following the new **Guidelines for Information Technology**, the organisation of automatic data processing (ADP) has been streamlined, *i.e.* in every department there is now only one organisational unit responsible for ADP. The use of ADP throughout the civil service is co-ordinated by a committee in the Federal Chancellery. Furthermore, a system of cost accounting has been introduced in the Federal Accounting Office and the introduction of an ADP programme evaluation system is in preparation.
- In the area of the **"space utilisation scheme for federal ministries"**, the Department of Administration of Federal Buildings became a privately-managed federal property company, the Federal Estate Agency, which is in charge of planning, financing and supervising the construction of buildings to be used by schools and universities (as a first step). Furthermore, all data necessary for optimum space utilisation are now being digitally recorded (CAD).
- In the field of **clerical systems, technical communication and documentation**, a new clerical system came into force on 1.1.1993. A handbook on Office Organisation in the Federal Administration, which describes those organisational steps required for the establishment of a modern result-oriented civil service office, was presented to the administration at large in February 1993. A special committee was created to assist in the implementation of the measures approved by the federal government.

Financial management

During 1993, **cost accounting** was introduced at the Austrian Central Office for Statistics and at the Federal Academy for Administration. Following a pilot project in evaluating the efficiency of personnel resources in the court system, the basic data for a controlling programme in one of the biggest administrative districts have been assembled. In some areas, costs of administrative performance have been calculated. Further guidelines for calculating the follow-up costs of legislation have been drawn up, and in every federal ministry a member of staff has been nominated to be specially responsible for the introduction of cost accounting. Comprehensive training programmes are now under way.

Management of human resources

The two pilot projects in the Ministry of Environment, Youth and Family and in the Ministry of Health, Sport and Consumer Protection are still under way. They are going to establish objectives, work out a corporate image and adapt their personnel planning accordingly, and develop and support senior executives in their careers in such a way that they can supervise career development among their staff.

Furthermore, a Job Exchange has been established within the Federal Chancellery, and has been in operation since the beginning of 1993. A system for a new performance-related pay scheme for civil servants, including elements of management by objectives, is under discussion.

Privatisation

In the field of privatising State activities, several new actions need to be mentioned. 1993 was the first operational year for the new **Federal Estate Agency** (BIG). Financing such activities (as mentioned above) in the private market shall significantly reduce construction time and thus create better cost-effectiveness in the public building sector.

Handing over the management of **cultural heritage** to private enterprise – albeit State-owned – has proved quite successful throughout0 1993. The new Schönbrunn Castle Company is making good progress towards a modern marketing of cultural resources, balanced by aspects of the necessary preservation of these resources. The company is well on its way to the final goal of being able to finance the necessary preservation investments by the net income of using Schönbrunn Castle and park as a museum and as a place of recreation and cultural events.

The necessary legislative measures for privatising **Austrian Railways** and the **Civil Aviation Administration** have been concluded. The implementation of re-organisation is on the way. At the moment, privatisation is also planned for the State-run telephone and postal services. Moreover, privatisation of labour exchange services will most likely be put into effect by the middle of 1994.

Organisational and structural change

The recent application by Austria for membership of the European Union has led to some fundamental discussions on the relative roles of the *Land* and the federal levels of government. These are likely to continue for the next few years. Following proposals for a new distribution of responsibilities, the preparations for a reform of the Constitution have begun. Political negotiations are under way.

BELGIUM

In 1993, findings from an in-depth study of personnel requirements (which provided an accurate picture of how each department was accomplishing its mission in terms of output relative to staff numbers, staff qualifications and patterns of organisation) were used:

– **At government level, to restructure the full range of services in the light of tasks to be accomplished. Aims of this structural adjustment review were:**
  – to adapt to transfers of responsibility to the Communities and Regions;
  – to ensure coherence with the responsibilities of the European Union;
  – to improve system links in the interests of better service to users;
  – to rationalise so as to improve efficiency by phasing out tasks which had become less relevant.

  It was thus decided on 29 July 1993 to establish the federal civil service as ten operational ministerial departments, together with a general administration department bringing together the general logistical services and the Prime Minister's services. Public agencies forming part of the federal civil service were also restructured, some being incorporated into ministerial departments.

  The new Ministry of General Administration will include sections dealing with personnel policy, training, organisation and computer consultancy, recruitment, property, supplies, medical monitoring and an auditing committee (Comité supérieur de contrôle).

  The College of Secretaries-General prepared a detailed draft of these new structures which was submitted to the Minister for the Civil Service on 4 November 1993. It is to be implemented in 1994 and 1995. It entails restructuring and departmental mergers.

  The government has also decided to extend the in-depth study to penitentiary establishments (completed in June 1993), diplomatic posts (completed in March 1994) and administrative staff of the Council of State (completed in January 1994), to the courts of justice (on-going) and to the police force (on-going).

  In addition to restructuring (some of it extensive), within individual ministries, attention should be drawn to a five-year plan for modernising the Ministry of Finance and a pluriannual plan for Justice, both of which were put in hand in 1993.

– **At the level of administrative and budgetary auditing, by an in-depth review of staffing needs based on system criteria associated with performance of tasks.**

  This takes the budget beyond a legal authorisation to make it more of a management instrument, applied practically in the preparation of budget decisions in July 1993 (for the 1994 budget). This aspect was strengthened by the new pluriannual character of budget proposals, guided by the plan to converge economic policies in member States of the European Union.

  New staff structures are also being put into effect, reflecting the results of the in-depth study and new administrative structures in so far as those are already operational.

  The exercise is also expected to include jobs at the new level created for holders of non-university higher education qualifications, to simplify careers (fewer hierarchy ranks) and to bring posts (permanent or temporary) back in line with the status (established or contractual) of officials holding them.

– **At the level of service managers, by focusing activities on what is essential and by re-organising working procedures and processes.**

The Civil Service Act of 22 July 1993 was amended to encourage greater mobility. One effect of mobility should be to enable each service to adjust its staff numbers according to the needs emerging from the in-depth study and the resulting decisions. It is proposed to establish a special unit within the General Administration Service to manage mobility.

Work began in 1993 on two substantial projects to implement the new general principles of the statute of civil service (Decree of November 1991). One of these relates to the **managerial appointments system** (fixed term, renewable once only in the same post), the other to **modernised staff appraisal.** These projects have still to be negotiated with staff representative organisations and approved by the political authorities.

Two Royal Decrees of September 1993 redefined and strengthened the **role of the College of Secretaries-General and managerial officials**. The College is a consultative body for all staff policy and departmental organisation proposals. Each Secretary-General has the task of allocating resources among his ministry's departments. In this connection, the Secretary-General manages general services, formulates the budget and oversees its implementation. Heads of administration deal directly with the minister on matters concerning their own departments.

The documentation base management group is working on an economic classification of expenditures and revenues in accordance with the European System of Integrated Economic Accounts (ESA) and on improving the quality of public finance statistics. Two Royal Decrees have established a **Public Accounts Standardisation Board** which was set up on 20 April 1993 and works on a double entry accounts system.

As regards **relations with the public**, the following developments may be mentioned for 1993:

- The Public Service Users' Charter was approved on 4 December 1992. The College of Secretaries-General is responsible for evaluating its implementation.
- A working group reviewed important administrative documents for their readability. Its report of July 1993 contains recommendations which the College of Secretaries-General will examine.
- Initiatives have been taken to create an information function within ministries and to organise open days for the public.
- A large-scale project to **simplify and improve the layout of forms**, called "Auditform", began in 1993. Results for those self-employed in small and medium-size enterprises are expected for end-1994.

CANADA

The past year has been an eventful one for the public service and for government overall in Canada.

Size and structure of the public sector

Reduction in resources

As part of the Government's strategy to control the deficit and to ensure strong economic growth, the Economic Statement of 2 December 1992 reduced operating costs for all departments by 3 per cent for the 1993/94 and 1994/95 fiscal years, and froze salaries of public servants for two years.

The Budget announced in April 1993 extended and reinforced the actions taken in the December Statement in order to yield combined savings of C$3.8 billion in 1993/94, rising to C$7.9 billion in 1997/98. Together these measures were expected to save C$30.7 billion.

The 1993 Budget included further streamlining measures. An additional 12 agencies, advisory boards and departments were eliminated or merged. The amalgamation of Taxation and Customs and Excise into a single Department of National Revenue was also announced as part of these measures. As well, it was announced that seven organisations were set aside to be considered for privatisation or commercialisation.

Government re-organisation of 25 June 1993

On 25 June 1993, Prime Minister Campbell announced a significant downsizing and restructuring of government. The Prime Minister indicated that new structures of government were necessary to respond to changing times and changing needs of Canadians, and to meet the demands of Canadians for more effective and responsive government. These factors, coupled with continuing pressures to streamline government, were the major forces behind the restructuring initiative.

The size of Cabinet was reduced from 35 to 25. All "Minister of State" positions were abolished, and the Cabinet decision-making system was streamlined to restore full Cabinet as **the** forum for decision-making. Six Cabinet committees were eliminated, including the Priorities and Planning Committee.

The restructuring affected all departments in the public service. The number of departments was reduced from 32 to 23: eight departments were created or fundamentally redesigned; three departments received additional mandates; and 15 departments were merged or wound up. All departments were asked to submit plans for administrative streamlining and for regional consolidation. As a result, the number of deputy ministers was reduced by 28 per cent and the number of assistant deputy ministers was reduced by 17 per cent (from 319 to 266).

New Government: 4 November 1993

The federal election held on 25 October 1993 resulted in a majority for the Liberal Party. The new Government took office on 4 November 1993. Prime Minister Chrétien announced a Cabinet of 23 ministers, down from 25.

The new Government introduced a major innovation, the appointment of eight Secretaries of State who, although part of the ministry, are not members of the Cabinet. This new position has been created to provide additional support to Cabinet ministers and to the Government as a whole. Secretaries of State are sworn to the Privy Council and as such they are bound by collective responsibility.

The Prime Minister also announced further streamlining of the Cabinet decision-making machinery. Full Cabinet is the senior forum for collective decision-making. In addition, there are four Cabinet committees:

- Economic Development Policy;
- Social Development Policy;
- Treasury Board;
- Special Committee of Council.

These changes are designed to make the Cabinet decision-making system simpler and faster.

Prime Minister Chrétien also announced changes to the government structure, notably the creation of a new Department of Citizenship and Immigration, and the re-establishment of the Department of the Solicitor General. As well, the Prime Minister appointed a minister with specific responsibilities for public service renewal. This appointment reflects the Government's commitment to a close and effective partnership between ministers and the public service and to a professional, non-partisan public service able to serve the needs of the Government and of all Canadians.

Central agencies

The 25 June re-organisation affected two central agencies. The **Privy Council Office** was given responsibility for federal-provincial relations, with the re-integration of the Federal Provincial Relations Office into the PCO. The functions of the Office of the Comptroller General were also integrated into the **Treasury Board Secretariat**.

Special operating agencies

Special operating agencies (SOAs) are operational organisations within existing departmental structures which deliver services, as distinct from providing policy advice. There are now 15 SOAs approved by the Treasury Board. Two more were announced in the 1993 Budget: Translation Services (which will become an SOA in 1995) and Surveys, Mapping and Remote Sensing. This means that there will soon be over 7 000 people employed in SOAs. In addition, a number of departments are working towards establishing SOAs, *e.g.* Realty Services and Architectural and Engineering Services at the Department of Public Works and Governmental Services.

Other areas of public management reform

Passage of Bill C-26: the Public Service Reform Act

A milestone in the renewal of the public service was reached when Bill C-26 was passed by Parliament in December 1992. It marked the first major overhaul of the legislation governing management of the public service in over a quarter of a century. This new legislative framework provided for many of the changes in human resources and administrative management described in the *Public Service 2000* White Paper, and was a key element in maintaining the momentum for renewal.

The Act contained amendments to the Public Service Employment Act, the Public Service Staff Relations Act, the Financial Administration Act, and the Surplus Crown Assets Act. The Act included provisions in areas such as the efficient deployment of employees, authority to simplify the job classification system and streamlining the staffing process. In addition, fair treatment of employees was enhanced as a result of new provisions on employment equity, the end of probation on appointments other than initial entry to the public service, and earlier union membership for term employees.

Personnel management

In July 1993, the Government imposed temporary controls on recruitment into the public service, to remain in effect indefinitely, in order to give priority to employees displaced by restructuring. Although a freeze was imposed, recruitment programmes aimed at rejuvenating the public service by recruiting top-notch graduates to joint its ranks – such as the Management Trainee Programme and the Accelerated Economists Training Programme – were exempted.

Information technology

In July 1993, the Government launched a major initiative to make better use of information technology in streamlining the delivery of services to Canadians and reducing the cost of administration. The focal point for driving the changes, which form part of the overall government restructuring process, was the establishment of the position of chief informatics officer (CIO) within the Treasury Board Secretariat. The CIO's mandate includes developing policy and standards related to information management and technology, exercising functional direction over departmental information management and technology, actively supporting re-engineering of government administrative processes and delivery mechanisms, and establishing partnerships with the private sector in this area.

Service to the public

The Government is placing a significant focus upon increased efficiency, effectiveness and accountability in the delivery of service to clients, both within government and directly to the Canadian public. Some of the examples of innovative service improvements to date are:

– **Canada Business Service Centres** respond to the business community's need for better service by bringing together information about the programmes and services available from over 12 departments and agencies into a single point of access. These centres, which can be reached by a toll-free number, have shown high levels of client satisfaction since their inception in 1992. Three such centres have been introduced to date in major centres (Edmonton, Winnipeg and Halifax) and more are planned.
– The **InfoCentre** initiative led by the Department of Human Resources Development has been implemented in almost 230 locations across the country to offer services and information to individual Canadians. Selected InfoCentres are also serving as rolling test-beds for innovative self-service. New sorts of partnership with other levels of government and the private sector are also being explored to enhance the benefits of InfoCentres.
– The **Electronic Procurement and Settlement System** at Public Works and Government Services is being redesigned to eliminate most of the costs associated with 80 per cent of the administration of these tasks. The procurement of goods and settlement of accounts will be handled electronically to reduce the paper burden for internal clients and private sector suppliers.

To meet the service expectations of the public, the public service needs a clear understanding within and outside government of the level of service to be provided. Under the leadership of the Treasury Board Secretariat, many departments have provided their clients with initial service standards for their services.

DENMARK

Commercialisation or corporatisation of public bodies

Actions were taken towards the **commercialisation and corporatisation of Danish State Railways**. During 1993, decisions were taken to enable Danish State Railways (DSB) to meet greater international transport competition in conformity with European Union transport policy and regulations, especially Council statute number 1893/91 and Commission directive number $^{91}/_{440}$ concerning the European railways. Major actions are:

- New legislation was passed late in 1993 implying the **separation of operational transport activities from regulatory and authority functions**. The chief executive officer of DSB no longer has direct access to the Minister of Transport as the DSB no longer has departmental status. Business is thus separated from politics.
- The former unified business of DSB has been changed into a new **corporate structure embracing a number of divisionalised business units**: rail infrastructure; passenger traffic; goods transport; ferries (Ltd); buses (Ltd); travelling bureau (Ltd). The latter three divisions will be turned into State-owned limited companies due to their competitive standing. Buses are likely to be changed first into a limited company. At present no decisions have been taken as to the possibility of partial or complete privatisation of these companies.
- The concept of political control of **corporate DSB is to be based on contract steering**. The Minister of Traffic will commit corporate DSB and its main units to the delivery of certain amounts and qualities of socially-needed transport services in return for certain levels of public grants. Contracts shall make subsidies transparent and allow for a high degree of business autonomy. Steering by contracts prepares for further commercialisation. However, no planning has yet been initiated on turning the core rail business into limited companies.

Management of policy-making

A **reform of the Prime Minister's Office** (PMO) was undertaken. During 1993, the PMO was expanded in size and restructured. Three major divisions have been established: the Division of International Affairs, the Division of National Policies, and the Division of Cabinet Matters. The restructuring is aimed at strengthening the Prime Minister's decision-making capacity and improving the co-ordinating function of the PMO.

Personnel management

For the first time a genuine **personnel policy** has been formulated for the State institutions. The policy stresses the need for working conditions which develop the skills, capacity and sense of responsibility of the employees. The policy demands that yearly formal evaluation talks take place between the employer and the local employees and that the individual public institution's personnel policy be evaluated at least every second year. The personnel policy, expressed by the Ministry of Finance, states that public employees ought to be involved in the formulation of goals and strategies for the individual institution. They should also be able to influence the organisation of the work.

Improving relations with citizens/enterprises

Development of a concept of service standard statements in the public sector was a theme of the Government's principal statement of June 1993 on the public sector. The Ministry of Finance is currently developing a common concept of service standards which can be used in different parts of the public service sector in various ways.

A public service standard statement is a short and clear description (or informative label) of the key features and standards of a public service. This form of consumer information may be presented as a declaration of contents of public services. Service standard statements may include information about service goals, performance results and the means of attaining redress. The service standards can provide users with information about what to expect from the public services delivered and what they are entitled to. Informing users about public services is a method for improving the quality of public service as the features of the public services become more transparent.

Partial privatisation of *"Postgiro"*

Privatisation was another, though minor, field of change in 1993. This is due to the continuing process of privatisation of the *"Postgiro"* postal banking and payment services. These were previously a business unit within the national State Post and Telecom Service. In January 1991, *"Postgiro"* was turned into a separate limited company heading for an agreed 25 per cent privatisation. However, in 1993 the Government and opposition agreed on an extended 51 per cent privatisation. Emission of shares was successfully completed at the Copenhagen Stock Exchange by the end of 1993.

FINLAND

General

The Government made a **Decision on Guidelines for Reforming the Central and Regional Administration** in June 1993. The decision focuses on structural changes and redefining the roles of different levels of government as well as increasing market orientation in the functioning of public authorities. Main lines in the structural changes are:

– Central government will be turned into a single-level system instead of the present two-level structure with strong central agencies.
– An increased number of government functions will be organised as public enterprises or companies.
– The role of regional authorities based on associations of municipalities will be strengthened and consequently authority transferred from State provincial offices to the municipality-based regional government, particularly in matters related to regional development.
– The State regional government will be streamlined and co-operation between various authorities increased.

Along the lines approved by the **Government Programme for Public Sector Reform** in May 1992, the work on improving productivity and quality of the public sector is under way and taking many forms.

Cutting public expenditure is a permanent and major concern of the Government. Major instruments in use are budget ceilings and the annual budget preparation procedure, whereby the innovations of the early 1990s are being consolidated.

The importance of international information on administrative reforms has been increasing. Recognising the need for information on international experiences, the Ministry of Finance conducted an **International Comparison Project** in 1992/93. The Project produced several sub-reports and a main report in Autumn 1993. The report includes comparative material on public management reforms in OECD countries and a collection of basic statistical data on public sectors in the OECD countries as well as an assessment of the present situation of the Finnish public sector and its reform. The Project proposed that an evaluation of the public sector reform policy since 1986 should be undertaken in Finland. The Project also proposed a new emphasis on regulatory management as a part of public sector reform strategy.

Size and structure of the public sector

Limits to the size of the public sector

The system of **budgetary ceilings**, introduced in 1990/91, has gained an established position as a political control instrument in budgeting. Changes to the original ceilings structure and procedures have been minor: the timetables have been made more flexible, and the sub-ceilings (*i.e.* those within ministries) have been given only an informative role. The budgetary process is now more delegated to the line ministries, who have succeeded rather well in adopting their new and difficult role as executors of cutbacks.

One means of adjusting the public sector is by **controlling the number of personnel** in the State administration. This method was used by the Government in 1989-91. The Government has set a target of reducing the number of State personnel by 6.8 per cent from 1992 to 1994. This control method will still be used up to 1996. The Government has decided to give up the method after that year.

In the State budget for 1994, the **State personnel costs will be reduced** by over 5 per cent. The reductions will be achieved both by the measures taken by individual agencies (3.5 per cent) and by central collective agreements (1.9 per cent). In 1993, the running costs of the State agencies were cut by 4 per cent. This was achieved by leaving posts unfilled, by saving part of vacation pay and, to a minor degree, by lay-offs.

Privatisation

There are only few cases of privatisation (for example, the State Personnel Restaurants were transformed into a private company in 1993), but its use depends on the situation in the capital market, which is expected to become more favourable in the future. In 1993, cases of privatisation were more frequent in the municipal sector than in the State sector.

Parliament has approved that Cabinet may give up the State ownership of two more public enterprises (the State Computer Centre, the Mint of Finland), and to reduce the degree of State ownership of five industrial companies (*e.g.* the national oil company, Neste Ltd).

Commercialisation and corporatisation of public bodies

The process of turning government units into public enterprises and companies is continuing. An enterprise is a way of organising service production calling for public control within a competitive situation. For activities in the fields where functioning market enterprises already exist, the alternative of turning the activity directly into a company will be considered.

In addition to earlier re-organisations, the Post and Telecommunications and some public building activities will be turned into joint-stock companies in 1994. Other similar re-organisations, concerning for example the State Railways, are also being prepared.

In 1993, a study evaluating new types of public enterprises was started. The report of this study will be published in Autumn 1994.

Decentralisation to sub-national government

The main objectives of decentralisation of public administration, initiated in the mid-1980s, are to increase flexibility, efficiency and effectiveness, and reduce and simplify administrative control systems. For these purposes, the ongoing work includes the following efforts:

- cutting the number of administrative levels both in central and regional administration by streamlining or abolishing central authorities and administrative bodies;
- eliminating duplication of duties, and delegating decision-making in all cases to the level of administration which provides the services or serves the clients. This means that, in the provision of services, a frontline policy will be adopted. In addition to the decentralisation of powers, less control will be exercised over the frontline;
- through **reforming the system of State subsidies to municipalities**, some regulations concerning the activities of municipalities (local authorities) have already been withdrawn or simplified. Also, the control and supervision systems of municipalities have undergone reforms. A number of rules, created by legislation or otherwise, regulating the provision of services and organisation of municipal activities are due to be repealed in 1994;
- **reducing and simplifying permit procedures:** only permits related to issues of national importance will be subject to approval by ministries and other central authorities. Permit procedures for other purposes will either be eliminated or transferred to local or regional administrations. The intention is to introduce these measures by the end of 1994;
- **reforming regional administration:** existing administrative units will be reduced in size or re-organised by combining several units. The availability of services will be guaranteed through this process. Services will be decentralised in order to increase the independence and influence of decision-making at the regional level;
- in accordance with the Regional Development Act (which will come into force from the beginning of 1994), **the main responsibility for regional development and the design of regional policies** will be delegated from State provincial offices (counties) to the regional councils (based on associations of municipalities). It is envisaged that different national authorities responsible for regional administration will be given powers to contribute to the preparation and implementation of regional development programmes under the direction of the regional councils.

Use of market-type mechanisms

Market-type mechanisms have been utilised in several ways. Unbiasing the cost of inputs is discussed below. The role of **user charges** has grown more important since the adoption of the 1992 Law on User Charges. The Government policy regarding buy-or-make decisions is to encourage market testing of all so-called support services and, in some cases, also final outputs of government agencies. Changing organisations into limited stock corporations or off-budget public enterprises and introducing net budgeting is being encouraged. Similar trends also apply to local authorities.

The possibilities for using market-type mechanisms have also been studied for some welfare services (*e.g.* using vouchers in children's day-care), and this line of development will be pursued further.

Other main fields of public management reform

Management of policy-making

To **develop the functioning of the General Session of the Cabinet**, legislation has been changed so that the division of authority between the General Session and the ministries will be more flexible from the beginning of 1994. The decision-making level will be defined according to the importance and scope of the matter. The reform also includes the re-organisation of decision-making powers within ministries. Delegation from the minister to civil servants will become more flexible.

A reform of the decision-making system of the Cabinet is under preparation. Traditionally, the system is based on written proposals. Both the written proposals and the memos appended to them are distributed to the ministers and their assistants before decisions are made. The annual volume of these materials is about 80 000 written pages.

To support the decision-making system, an automatic data processing system will be introduced as from the beginning of 1995. All materials within the Cabinet decision-making system will be in electronic form. The new system will provide, for example, the following advantages: acquaintance with forthcoming matters in advance, the preparation of session agendas, electronic communication between Cabinet and Parliament, and the production of the minutes of sessions.

Performance management

In 1993, the running costs of a majority of agencies were budgeted according to the **results-oriented budgeting** paradigm. Experiences have so far been encouraging: the agencies budgeted by results have been able to adjust to the present financial difficulties of the Government, and have shown an average of 9 per cent unused balances for 1992. This has presented the line ministries with a dilemma: whether to claim back those balances to meet the ever-tightening ceilings, or to let the agencies keep them as reserves.

The results-oriented approach to budgeting has been applied to **transfers** to a very limited extent so far. Non-agricultural subsidies have been subject to some interesting studies, and the Ministry of Trade and Industry is working to reduce their cost and improve their effectiveness. Transfers to households are a more difficult case. The reform of State subsidies to local authorities, enacted at the beginning of 1993, relaxed most central government controls on local authorities' State-subsidised services, thus allowing them to apply more rational, results-oriented budgeting and management practices as well as to rely more on market mechanisms.

Mainly due to their difficult financial situation, quite important progress is being made in numerous local authorities both as regards determination of political priorities and the introduction of new management techniques in health, social services, education and technical services.

The problems which remain in results-oriented budgeting are numerous, however, and range from political problems of setting priorities to measuring results at the agency level, and to coping with incentives for managers and other civil servants. To improve present practices in results-oriented management, the Ministry of Finance has set up a project which concentrates on the methodological development of results-oriented management in the ministries.

The Government Programme for Public Sector Reform emphasizes the need for better quality and productivity of public services. For this, the Ministry of Finance has set up a **Quality and Productivity Project** aiming at supporting and encouraging line ministries to start an active quality and productivity policy in their respective service and policy sectors. All ministries have been required to draw up a quality and productivity programme for the end of the 1990s. The initiative aims at strengthening performance-oriented management procedures and making target-setting more viable and more clearly oriented towards better productivity and quality.

The Project has started pilot programmes in various service sectors (the police, administrative courts, employment services). It has also published general guidelines for quality management and cost control methods in the public sector.

The Project has also demonstrated that various quality management techniques, such as service delivery standards, could be used as an alternative to detailed regulation of public service production. Research and assessment of the possibilities for using quality standards in the management of welfare services has been started.

Financial resources management

The **Budget Decree** has been completely rewritten to reflect the new constitutional provisions concerning State finances and the corresponding changes in the Budget Law, and enacted as of the beginning of 1993. The decree gives new instructions, for example on ministerial management of agencies by results, on submission of annual closed accounts and activity reports of agencies to the ministries, and on the rate of return requirements of capital assets of the State.

Further reform work on the **Budget Law** is about to be completed by a working group nominated by the Minister of Finance. The draft proposal for the Budget Law will reform the State accounting system to be more accrual-based, and will fine-tune existing rules to take better account of the new constitutional provisions and experiences with their implementation. The Bill planned to be submitted to Parliament in late 1993 should be enacted as a law at the beginning of 1995.

The process of **unbiasing cost attribution** started in 1991 with the introduction of a pensions charge on the wages and salaries of agencies. The process will continue with the introduction of a system of charging **market-level rent for State-owned office premises** in 1994 and for other premises in 1995. After that, there will still remain certain costs related to the use of capital that are not attributed to agencies (interest charge on non-fixed assets and cash requirements, certain asset-related service charges), where only the calculated rate-of-return requirement is applied.

The Cabinet and Parliament accepted a general guideline in connection with the 1992 amendment of the Budget Law. This adjusts **government accounting** to business accounting where it is practical to do so. The Ministry of Finance, in co-operation with the State Treasury and several pilot agencies, has started a major development project, where accrual concepts are tested and problems are identified and solved with the aim of getting an essentially accrual accounting system into government-wide use starting from 1995. Parallel work has been done on legislation in the working group mentioned above.

In addition, the State Committee on Local Authorities is working on accounting reform in local authorities with the aim of adopting regular business accounting starting from 1997.

Personnel management

As a consequence of structural reforms and rationalisation measures, some State personnel become redundant. Most of these people can be displaced elsewhere within the State administration. A small number have, however, been given notice. Special efforts have been made to redirect those without work by encouraging them to retrain themselves, to find a new workplace, or to become entrepreneurs. In June 1993, the Government made a decision on the principles to be followed in the **displacement of personnel**. According to this decision, agencies have the responsibility for displacement according to general guidelines set by ministries. In addition to displacement, the competencies of personnel in labour markets are improved and support for re-employment is offered. The displacement measures of agencies are supported by special grants in the State budget.

The Project on the Reform of the Legal Status and Employment of State Personnel, initiated in 1991, has been completed, and the proposal for **new civil service legislation** is before Parliament. The goal of the new legislation is to create employment categories which promote effective and appropriate performance in different task areas and fulfil the needs for legal security.

The intent of the proposed legislation is that differences between the civil service and the State employee categories should be reduced. Only the differences necessitated by the nature of tasks should remain between the two categories. The possibility of individual agreements with civil servants is proposed. The intention is that the civil service category should be used basically in the agencies included in the State budget, whereas the employee category should be used basically in State enterprises.

Simultaneously with the reform of civil service legislation, the **system of collective bargaining and agreements** has been reformed. The structure of civil service collective agreements has been renewed for the next agreement period. The goal concerning wages and salaries is to reinforce the system of agreements at the agency level and to improve the possibilities for executing a results-oriented wage policy in the agencies. To a certain degree, the agencies can reform their wage systems and terms of employment for civil servants. As earlier, the payment of State employees is agreed in the individual agencies. In the agreements at the central level, general orders for agreements in the agencies are approved.

The **Association of State Enterprise Employers** was set up in March 1993. This Association represents the interests of new State enterprises and related joint stock companies as employers. The founders of the Association were: Post and Telecommunications, State Railways, National Civil Aviation Organisation, Motor Vehicles Registration Centre, State Computer Centre Ltd, and the Ministry of Finance. All new State enterprises and companies reformed from them have joined the Association. There are about 60 000 employees in the service of the member enterprises of the Association.

The establishment of the Association is connected with the broader re-organisation of State employer activities. The organisation for agreements and employer interests of State enterprises is being distinguished in a functional way from the corresponding organisation for the agencies in the State budget. This implies that the field of State collective agreements is divided into two independent sub-areas which are united by the general outlines for the personnel policies of the State.

The Ministry of Finance has carried out two development and training programmes for top management: 25 top managers from both the public administration and enterprises participated in the **"Development Programme of National Strategy"** in 1993. Thus, all 100 of the top managers have participated in the Programme in 1992/93. In addition, 100 managers and senior experts from State administration also participated in the **"Development Programme of Public Management"**.

Special emphasis in personnel and management development has been put on **training for European integration**. The training aims to achieve the goal that everyone in the service of the State has the basic information on European integration and the language ability needed in his/her job. The purpose is to secure the national interests in the best way, to have high-level civil servants for different tasks in the European Union, and to ensure that the domestic administration is well prepared.

The Ministry of Finance has set up a **Development of Work Units Project** which aims to identify the important factors for productivity and well-being of personnel in work units. The project will be completed by the end of 1994 and will search for general ways of problem-solving and spread information on models considered relevant. The project is undertaking concrete sub-projects in 30 different agencies of the State.

In addition, a project set up by the Ministry of Finance has developed a scenario entitled the **"Management of State Concern in 2000"**. The project chose for the basis of development the principles of openness, flexibility, responsibility and effectiveness as managerial values. The Ministry of Finance has started a project which aims to improve systematic **personnel development** of the State by serving better the functional strategies of the agencies. The project has started sub-projects in different agencies.

Improving relations with citizens/enterprises

The **Service Project**, initiated in 1989, has been completed and its final report published in December 1993. The report summarises the work and results of the Project, and proposes new efforts for the improvement of services: increasing the joint use of public resources in customer service and in administrative support services, promoting the dissemination of information on services, developing results-oriented management to include agreements on requirements for service standards, and creating new market-based service production by competition.

The comprehensive Citizen's Guide to public services was edited into electronic form in 1993.

Management of information technology

The amount of data to be collected by public authorities will be reduced. Data systems and statistics will be combined and simplified so as to ensure that as a rule the same data are collected only once. Data systems will be developed according to co-ordinated principles, using general classifications.

A **government information management strategy** will be drawn up by the end of 1993. It is being designed to guide the future development of the data systems used by various government branches and various departments and agencies.

A **national information management strategy**, designed to promote the development of information technology in different sectors, and taking into account national and international needs, will also be drawn up by the end of 1994. The strategy is being developed in co-operation with different ministries, universities and private enterprises.

References

Government of Finland (1993*a*), *Government Decision-in-Principle on Reform in Central and Regional Government, June 17, 1993*, Helsinki (a draft version is available in English).

Government of Finland (1993*b*), *Tietoja valtion henkilöstöstä 1970-1992* (Data on the Personnel of the State 1970-1992), Helsinki (only in Finnish).

Ministry of Finance (1993*a*), *Maailman paras julkinen sektori?* (The World's Best Public Sector?), the final report of the International Comparison Project, Helsinki (only in Finnish; a partial translation in English is available).

Ministry of Finance (1993*b*), *Tuloksena palvelu* (The Result is Service), final report of the Service Project, Helsinki (only in Finnish).

FRANCE

Public sector trends

The incoming government of April 1993 aimed to strengthen and consolidate the long-established policy of adapting public services to contemporary needs, rather than introduce many new measures.

Public management continued against a background of wage restraint and controlled staff numbers and costs, as part of government's objective of redressing public deficits (in the budget, and also in welfare accounts). With this aim in view, Parliament enacted a Public Finances Act during its Autumn 1993 session which should enable France to meet the 1997 target date for the Maastricht treaty's convergence criteria, bringing its budget deficit down to 3 per cent of GDP by 1996 and 2.5 per cent by 1997, and also stabilising the debt at 42 per cent of GDP in 1996, assuming growth rates of 2.7 per cent from 1995 onwards.

The fourth annual set of measures provided for under the 1990 Agreement on civil service pay scale adjustment was implemented in accordance with government commitments in 1990. A further agreement covering 1994/95, entered into by five civil service unions on 9 November 1993, will preserve the purchasing power of civil servants in real terms. This comprehensive agreement not only covers pay scales as such but also provisions designed to speed up civil service recruitment, proposals for part-time work and certain welfare measures.

In addition, there has been more emphasis on the social mediation role which the public service can play as an instrument serving the general public, on what it can contribute to land-use planning, on the cohesion which central government needs to ensure ten years after the sweeping decentralisation reform, and on strengthening an appropriately structured presence of central government in France and of France in Europe.

Creation of companies, enterprises, establishments

One of the Finance Ministry's central administrative bodies, the National Printing Directorate, has been re-organised as a limited company whose equity is 100 per cent State-owned.

Some civil service departments have been transformed into public establishments (*établissements publiques*) to make them more independent and efficient. The departments concerned cover training (*écoles supérieures*), cultural matters (museums etc.) and health (supply of blood, medicines etc.).

The Post Office and *France Télécom* are independent operations which have been linked to the State by contracts (*contrats de plan*) since the reforms of 1 January 1991: during 1993, the question of making them more independent was under intensive review.

Privatisation

In 1993 three State enterprises were privatised. One was an industrial company, the two others were banks.

Introduction of commercial practices

All publicly operated service providers continued to carry out surveys and discuss ways of developing up-to-date management techniques, without prejudicing the basic principles and approaches which uniquely characterise a public service.

Other main fields of public management reform

Administrative deconcentration

The main thrust of reform in 1993 was **administrative deconcentration**. This policy is based in law on the Territorial Administration Act of 6 February 1992 and the Deconcentration Charter Decree of 1 July 1992. It was needed in order to improve service quality for the public by introducing "close-to-hand" services, to improve government machinery, (through new management methods and in particular, giving civil servants greater personal responsibility) and to develop successful partnerships between the State and local communities.

These transfers of responsibility within the State are expected to prompt re-organisation in central government machinery, and to tailor deconcentrated services more closely to needs by strengthening co-ordination among services (poles of competence) under the authority of the *préfet*.

To this effect and following preparatory consultations in 1992, the government's Interministerial Committee for Territorial Administration decided on 23 July 1993 to produce four-year ministerial guidelines for each ministry's re-organisation and deconcentration, by early 1994. The guidelines would not only set targets but also determine the new patterns of organisation, the staffing and financial resources, and information flow, monitoring and evaluation procedures. Guidelines for each ministry would be devised by a steering committee consisting of representatives from central government and from deconcentrated services, including one *préfet* and one financial controller.

In parallel, three priorities were selected, namely updating financial procedures in response to growing deconcentration, tailoring auditing methods to match stronger deconcentrated powers, and boosting local services with high-calibre staff.

Preparing the new guidelines dovetailed with work begun several years earlier on developing participatory management, managers' performance appraisal and contractualisation between services and central government. To date over 700 service projects and 207 centres of responsibility have come into being. Their effectiveness is to be reviewed in 1993 and 1994.

Administrative location policy

Administrative location policy is one component in land use planning policy. On 12 July 1993 an Interministerial Territorial Planning Committee restated aims and general principles. It appreciably improved the implementing arrangements (concertation, welfare compensation scheme) and set a priority target of relocating 30 000 jobs from the greater Paris area to the provinces by the year 2000. Administrative location policy is to be co-ordinated with policy to modernise the public service through deconcentration.

In order to prevent over-manning, each of the ministries concerned will produce a job reclassification scheme for staff members not volunteering to transfer. When a staff member cannot be reclassified within his own ministry, transfer proposals will be put forward on an interministerial basis.

Improving the quality and effectiveness of public services in disadvantaged neighbourhoods

To improve quality of life for residents in disadvantaged neighbourhoods, the authorities and Parliament have been involved in an extensive range of seminars and discussions on urban and land-use planning, looking ahead to the year 2015.

To implement the inter-ministerial and inter-service policies needed more readily, budgeting and accounts management have been simplified, especially by cutting the number of budget lines and aggregating credits. Procedures whereby officials in different public services can co-operate with one another have been vigorously encouraged.

New financial incentives have been introduced to encourage officials to work in disadvantaged suburban areas and in depopulating rural cantons. Upon a recommendation of 29 July 1993 by the Inter-ministerial Committee on cities, supply and demand for public services will be more closely reviewed in disadvantaged areas so as to ease the adjustment process.

Appropriate adaptation measures for maintaining public services in rural areas, for which the Ministry of the Public Service is responsible, will strengthen existing consultation procedures, especially as *département*-wide public service guidelines are introduced, while innovation and experiment are relied upon to broaden officials' experience.

Improving citizen-administration relationships and better reception facilities for users

The first review of the Public Service Charter – adopted in March 1992 to underline the user's central position in public services, the principles underlying public service and its new measures – has been commented on by the Council of State and the Economic and Social Council. The review, together with their comments, will be put before Parliament. The nature of the Charter will be reconsidered in 1994.

Measures will be taken at national level to implement the conclusions of an evaluation of how disadvantaged groups are being served (training for officials, broadening their capabilities, assistance to services in evaluating demand and user satisfaction, etc.).

Apprenticeship

Under an Act of 17 July 1992, young people may now be offered apprenticeship contracts in the public services, using the voluntary services of officials acting as instructors.

GREECE

Size and structure of the public sector

Some deconcentration within central government has been achieved through the delegation of executive responsibilities from the central administration to prefects. Privatisation and limits to the size of the public sector have continued by maintaining the freeze on appointments and recruitment. Other restructuring/"rationalisation" efforts are contained in the Programme of Administrative Modernisation 1993-95, as mentioned in the 1993 Survey. Many measures adopted for the fulfilment of the reform goals, priorities and policies described in the 1993 Survey were still in progress in 1993.

Other main fields of public management reform

The field of personnel management has seen the application of the new system of administrative hierarchy as well as the new system for promotion in the public administration. A new performance appraisal system is being applied. An objective system of transfers based on quantitative data has been established.

Several measures to improve relations with citizens have been implemented. These include: the establishment of a single form to address to each administrative service; and extension of the network for administrative information to cover the entire country.

ICELAND

Budgeting and financial management

In the past three years, total government outlays have been reduced by 7 per cent in real terms. The reforms that were made to the budgeting and financial management systems, as outlined in last year's Survey, played a key role in achieving that reduction in outlays.

As input controls are relaxed, it is believed essential to establish standards for outputs. Pilot projects have been established between the Ministry of Finance and five line ministries on developing such standards. It is also under study how appropriations can be linked directly to outputs, *i.e.* appropriation on a per unit basis or on a defined project basis.

The Ministry of Finance is also studying the feasibility of introducing cost of capital charges whereby ministries and agencies would pay a certain charge to the Treasury based on the amount of capital they employ.

Privatisation

The government's privatisation programme continued actively in 1993. The sale of the Treasury's minority shareholding in *Íslensk endurtrygging* (re-insurance company) was finalised in June. *Síldarverksmidjur ríkisins* (herring processing) was privatised in December following corporatisation in March. *Sementsverksmidja ríkisins* (cement manufacturer) was corporatised in April in preparation for later privatisation.

The Treasury also announced its intention to sell the minority shareholding in *Thormódur rammi hf.* (trawlers and fish processing) and to corporatise and privatise *Lyfjaverslun ríkisins* (pharmaceutical manufacturer and distributor). These sales are planned for early 1994.

The Cabinet approved formal **"Guidelines for Privatisation"** in October. These guidelines define the roles of the Cabinet Committee on Privatisation, the Task Force on Privatisation and the relevant ministries. The guidelines mandate that all technical work, including valuation and execution of sale, be carried out by outside securities firms. The guidelines detail the steps to be followed in a trade sale and a public share offering. All special privileges enjoyed by, and duties imposed upon, companies are to be eliminated prior to sale. The promotion of competitive markets is a key objective of the government's privatisation programme; the guidelines permit the rejection of a highest bid in a trade sale if such a sale would lessen competition. The guidelines also aim to illuminate the privatisation process by requiring all companies to be widely advertised for sale as well as requiring detailed reports of each sale to be given to the public.

Regulatory reform

The Prime Minister appointed a Commission on Regulatory Reform in September. The Commission is to make recommendations on how to lighten the regulatory burden on individuals and corporations by streamlining the government's regulatory agencies and their activities.

A special feature of Iceland's regulatory reform programme is the privatisation of the inspection function of regulatory agencies whereby an agency will specify the standards to which an individual/enterprise must be held but leaving the actual inspections to private firms. This scheme has already been implemented on a limited basis.

Procurement

The Cabinet adopted a special **procurement policy** in September. The aim of this policy is to further increase the share of products, services and capital projects that are purchased/contracted by tender. The policy calls for all contracts for goods and services valued at IKr 2 million (US$30 000) or more to be made by competitive bid and all contracts for capital projects valued at IKr 5 million (US$70 000) or more to be made by competitive bid. These low monetary ceilings are in line with the government's ambitious targets for increasing procurement by competitive bid. The procurement policy also contains guidelines on the conduct of the State's procurement activities.

IRELAND

Size and structure of the public sector

Limits to the size of the public sector

Through formal decisions taken in the context of its consideration of the annual Estimates, the Government maintained its rigid policy on staffing in the civil service and non-commercial State bodies.

Privatisation

There were no significant developments in this area. The State relinquished further share holdings in two commercial State bodies, Irish Life (insurance company) and Greencore (sugar company) during the course of 1993.

Commercialisation or corporatisation of public bodies

Legislation was passed in Parliament during 1993 to create a new commercial State company, the Irish Aviation Authority. The body came into operation on 1 January 1994. The functions of this new body were formerly discharged within the civil service by the Air Navigation Services Office of the Department of Transport, Energy and Communications.

Decentralisation to sub-national government

Regulations were made which dispensed with various statutory controls under which local authorities were obliged to obtain consent, approval, confirmation and the like from the Minister for the Environment in performing specified statutory functions. These functions affected certain land disposals, delegation of functions by managers, local contributions to certain bodies, local authority superannuation, car parks, certain local authority meetings, and other matters.

An order was made increasing the range of functions reserved to the elected members of local authorities.

Provision was made in the Road Traffic Bill, which was before Parliament in 1993, for increased local authority responsibility and discretion in traffic management and the fixing of speed limits on the non-national roads.

In their *Programme for a Partnership Government*, the new *Fianna Fail*/Labour coalition Government announced that new county enterprise boards (counties are the basic unit of local government in Ireland) would be empowered to seek funding to assist local development, the start-up of small enterprises, and the promotion of tourism, and to establish community employment schemes in consultation with community organisations, the social partners and the public sector at local level.

Deconcentration within central government

1993 marked the final year of the first cycle of the administrative budget system, whereby civil service departments and offices are given considerable autonomy in the context of a three-year budget, which includes reductions in real terms in each of the three years, from which to manage their administrations (*e.g.* staff costs, office equipment, engagement of consultants, postal and telecommunications services, etc.). The purpose of these budgets is two-fold: to reduce the administrative costs of the civil service; and to afford local managers a greater degree of autonomy in the management of their administrations. During the latter half of 1993, new administrative budgets covering the period 1994-96 were negotiated by the Department of Finance with the various departments and offices. These new budgets incorporate a number of refinements and other improvements, compared to the previous budgets, which were inspired by the experience of the first cycle of administrative budgeting. It is intended that this second phase of the initiative should involve a greater delegation of autonomy for line managers within departments and offices.

New roles for central management bodies

In consequence of the evolution of the administrative budget system, the role of central management bodies is undergoing change. In the Department of Finance, which has relinquished a significant level of direct control over areas of administrative expenditure in civil service departments and offices, greater attention is now being focused on, *inter alia*:

- consultation with departments/offices operating the administrative budget system to help them in overcoming difficulties experienced in the introduction and development of the system;
- the consideration of such "macro" issues as grading structures, the benefits and drawbacks associated with the current usage level of consultants, international comparisons, etc.;
- those areas of administrative expenditure which have not been delegated to departments, particularly proposals concerning staffing at senior levels in departments/offices and major information technology projects.

For central management in those departments applying the administrative budget system, the challenge has been:

- to assume greater responsibility for the disposition of administrative resources within their own departments/offices while at the same time;
- encouraging managers in the various line divisions to take control of those elements of the administrative budget which are proper to their own areas.

Other restructuring or "rationalisation" efforts

The new coalition Government decided upon a considerable number of organisational changes across the public sector.

Civil service

A new Office of the *Tánaiste* (Deputy Prime Minister) was established. The Department of Energy was abolished, the forestry function transferring to the Department of Agriculture, Food and Forestry, while the residual energy functions were transferred to the Department of Tourism, Transport and Communication which was renamed as the Department of Transport, Energy and Communications and its previous tourism functions were transferred to the new Department of Trade and Tourism whose foreign trade functions were assigned from the Department of Industry and Commerce. The latter was renamed as the Department of Enterprise and Employment and acquired all the functions of the old Department of Labour save those relating to equality. The Department of Labour was renamed as the Department of Equality and Law Reform and received its law reform functions from the Department of Justice. Matters relating to the arts were transferred from the Department of the *Taoiseach* (Prime Minister) and broadcasting affairs from the Department of Tourism, Transport and Communications, to the Department of the *Gaeltacht* (the department charged with the development of Irish-speaking regions in the country) which was renamed as the Department of Arts, Culture and the *Gaeltacht*.

Non-commercial State bodies

Two initiatives were taken in 1993: an independent Environmental Protection Agency was established, and the Irish Film Board was reactivated.

Other

Finally, the National Economic and Social Forum was set up to contribute to the formation of a national consensus on major issues of economic and social policy and to the development of new initiatives to tackle unemployment. The Forum is representative of the social partners, organisations representing the unemployed, women's groups, the disadvantaged, and people with a disability.

Other main fields of public management reform

Management of policy-making

The Government is involved in ongoing talks with public service unions, which, it is intended, will lead to a restructuring of the existing grading system. Among the advantages which should accrue from such restructuring are: greater flexibility within the grading system leading to a breaking down of rigid divisions between grades and more streamlined administrative procedures.

Financial resources management

The Comptroller and Auditor General (Amendment) Act passed into law in 1993. The effect of the Act is to consolidate and update, as well as extend the range and scope of, the existing statutory provisions relating to the role of the Comptroller and Auditor General (C&AG). The most significant new provisions of the Act are as follows:

- all non-commercial State bodies, certain other publicly-funded bodies, health boards, vocational education committees and universities which have not heretofore been statutorily audited by the C&AG will now fall within his ambit;
- the C&AG will be empowered to carry out, at his discretion, examinations of the economy and efficiency of operation of departments and bodies which he audits; he is also empowered to examine the adequacy of the management systems which such bodies have in place to enable them to appraise the effectiveness of their own operations. A working group, representing the Department of Finance and the Office of the Comptroller and Auditor General, is preparing proposals for changes in financial reporting by government departments.

Most of the provisions of this new legislation did not come into operation until 1 January 1994.

In addition, progress has been maintained in the establishment of new financial management systems within departments/offices.

Personnel management

During 1993, the emphasis has been on consolidating the initiatives taken in the previous few years.

Regulatory management and reform

In April 1993, the Minister for Enterprise and Employment set up a Task Force to draw up a charter for small business under the chairmanship of the Minister of State (junior minister) for Commerce and Technology. In May a Technical Group of civil servants was established to assist and advise the Task Force in its consideration of the many matters of detail being reviewed. The regulatory demands made by State agencies – such as the Revenue Commissioners, Department of Social Welfare, Central Statistics Office, and Health and Safety Authority – on the small business sector are one of the areas being looked at as part of this exercise. The Technical Group has made a comprehensive trawl of agency compliance requirements and has collected and summarised details of regulations and forms used by departments and offices with a view to simplification and rationalisation. The Task Force is due to report early in March 1994.

The reduction of the cost of public services is being effected chiefly through the programme of administrative budgeting (see above), the second three-year cycle of which begins in 1994. The creation of a greater cost consciousness – a corollary to the establishment of administrative budgets – has also been facilitated by the ongoing development of financial management systems in the civil service.

Improving relations with citizens/enterprises

Many of the departments and offices which have direct dealings with the public have, in recent years, been developing programmes to improve customer relations. A significant development was taken in June 1993 by the Department of Social Welfare when it put in place electronic fund transfer (EFT) facilities for old-age contributory and retirement pensioners. EFT payments can be made either to a bank or a post office account. EFT is part of the Department of Social Welfare's strategy of offering a choice of payment methods to clients; it is cheaper and more efficient and can be safer, particularly for elderly clients.

In the *Programme for a Partnership Government*, a commitment was made to review the Patients' Charter so as to ensure that it provides a properly structured system of patients' rights. An undertaking to extend the remit of the Ombudsman to cover patients' rights was also made in the Programme. The Department of Health is currently considering how best these commitments may be fulfilled.

Management of information technology

At end 1993, the Central Computer Bureau, which provided mainframe computer facilities to a number of civil and public service bodies, was closed down after some twenty years of operation. The closure of the Bureau was a consequence of both changing technologies and the pursuit since the mid-1980s of a devolved, planning-driven approach to the provision of IT services within the Irish civil service. This resulted in individual government departments and offices acquiring in-house facilities to process and support their IT systems. The closure, which was effected over the three-year period 1991-93, involved the redesign and redevelopment of a number of major systems and the transfer of others to local departmental installations.

Though the Bureau service has ceased to operate, the Central IT Services of the Department of Finance continue to set overall policy for IT in terms of technical directions and strategies as well as providing advice and systems development support to other government departments and offices. They support also "common" administrative systems, such as payroll, personnel and financial systems, and the voice and data telecommunications infrastructure.

Other

On 20 May 1993, the *Access to Information on the Environment Regulations 1993* were made by the Minister for the Environment. Under these regulations, information relating to the environment, other than information held in connection with or for the purposes of any judicial or legislative function, or information which is already available to the public under any other enactment, is to be made available to any person without that person having to prove an interest.

In the *Programme for a Partnership Government*, a commitment was made to consider the introduction of freedom of information legislation which would enable the citizen the right of access to government papers generally (with exceptions for certain categories of sensitive information). Proposals in this regard are at an advanced stage of preparation.

The *Programme for a Partnership Government* also included a commitment to introduce legislation to enable parliamentary committees the right to compel the attendance and co-operation of witnesses and to confer on such witnesses absolute privilege in respect of any statements which they may make to such committees. The purpose of such legislation would, *inter alia*, be to make the activities of government more accessible to the public through the agency of parliamentary committees; the majority of witnesses before parliamentary committees tend to be civil servants. Draft legislation was submitted to the Parliamentary Draftsman before the end of 1993.

ITALY

Reform of public service regulations

Italy is undergoing a major process of change in the way its public administration and staff management system is organised. For the most part this will affect the status of civil servants, putting them in the same category as private sector employees and therefore subject to Civil Code regulations and negotiations with the unions. The only exceptions are magistrates (ordinary, administrative and financial), barristers and district attorneys, military personnel, police officers, diplomatic personnel, prefectural staff, and directors-general.

Enabling Act No. 421, passed on 23 October 1992, lays down provisions to rationalise public administrations and reform public service regulations.

The main lines of this reform, implemented under Ordinance No. 29 of 3 February 1993 are as follows:

- introducing a comparable relationship between labour competitiveness in the public sector, the private sector and the rest of Europe, with a view to introducing market forces into the public administration both at national and European level. This stems from the private sector's growing interest in investing in community services, and the increasing mobility of people and firms within the EU;
- as part of the policy to improve public finance required by European convergence and the instability of the currency market, bringing public sector labour costs in line with those of the private sector, and with those of corresponding public services in the rest of Europe. This means that any evaluation of staffing requirements in individual offices and government departments should take into account the total number of civil servants in the public administration; that salaries should be performance-related; and that average salaries should be set in relation to the overall wage bill and no longer be a free variable;
- individual accountability for programme performance, starting with managers who have clearly defined responsibilities for resource management and spending, as opposed to politicians who are responsible for defining which programmes will be undertaken and by whom, setting their budgets and checking their results. The new legislation does in fact define managerial duties in greater detail, clearly distinguishing them from the duties incumbent on politicians and giving managers similar autonomous authority over expenditure as part of their full managerial powers, the latter being largely free of any prior control by the Audit Office (*cour des comptes*);
- substantial flexibility with regard to:
    - *a)* organisational matters regarding services and the staff required to run them;
    - *b)* staff matters, namely allocating posts; assigning duties, possibly not in line with a person's skills; setting working hours; determining salaries, for the most part performance-related;
    - *c)* expenditure corresponding to the exclusive responsibilities of managers, according to their resource management powers and general performance;
- trade-union democracy, which means genuine debate between all parties. This should be the sole basis for salary regulations drawn up through collective bargaining, provided that the unions acknowledge that managers have autonomous responsibilities and users have rights, that they themselves are accountable as labour representatives for Italy's public and private sectors, and that they relate positively to the reality of the situation in Europe as a whole;
- establishing a new Agency for labour/union relations in the public administration, answering to the President of the Council of Ministers, and responsible for representing the administration in the collective bargaining process.

As part of the policy for financial recovery, public salaries were frozen until 31 December 1993 at the levels prevailing on 1 January 1992. It was also decided to postpone until 1 January 1994 the effects of new salary negotiations.

Moreover, Italy has for some years now been taking steps to reduce civil service recruitment by replacing only 25 per cent of staff retiring from local government and 10 per cent retiring from other parts of the administration.

Economic and financial strategy for 1994

The 1994 budget exercise includes steps to rationalise structures and operations in the public service, with a view to containing growth and enhancing human resource management, thereby increasing the productivity and efficiency of public institutions over the long term.

The structural rationalisation exercise will involve:

– eliminating obsolete or duplicate bodies which cause delays and raise the costs of administrative actions (*e.g.* review of out-lying organisations in the Ministry of Labour and closure of the Ministry of Merchant Marine);
– reducing interference between institutions to speed up their actions (*e.g.* eliminating numerous interministerial committees);
– scaling down the public administration by closing down public corporations (*établissements publiques*) and re-allocating the work of some other establishments;
– setting up internal performance monitoring;
– creating independent bodies for the allocation of public services.

With respect to staff, there are plans to rationalise the use of human resources, encourage the redeployment of public employees and increase productivity levels, by drawing up co-ordinated rules on appropriate staffing levels on the basis of workload studies, regulated turn-over and mobility management:

– Up to 31 December 1996, bodies in the public administration will be allowed to fill 5 per cent of posts falling vacant, first with surplus staff, next through mobility schemes (staff from other parts of the administration), and only then through the recruitment of new staff but with a ceiling of 10 per cent, and with proof of absolute necessity.
– When public employees are found to be surplus to requirements (after the reform/merger of parts of the public administration or the privatisation of public corporations, or due to workload studies) they are given leave of absence with an allowance equal to 80 per cent of their basic salary and the supplementary allowance, with a ceiling of L 1 500 000 (gross) per month. Leave of absence is cancelled if the employee is moved to another part of the administration under the mobility scheme.

The prime objective of the work carried out by the public administration is to eliminate excessive costs – generated by corruption or lack of efficiency – by renegotiating supply contracts for goods and services and for public works.

The objective where decision-making is concerned is to eliminate the invisible costs incurred through red tape. This is done by:

– reducing administrative delay times;
– lightening the burden of paperwork for individuals and firms;
– encouraging liberalisation by increasing the number of activities that can be undertaken upon simple declaration to the relevant part of the administration;
– setting up interdepartmental conferences to simplify complex administrative procedures involving several departments.

This strategy for the civil service was announced in the programme presented to Parliament by Prime Minister Ciampi's government. It is part of a drive to modernise the public administration proposed by the current Minister for the Civil Service, Mr. Sabino Cassese. Its main thrusts can be summarised by the following recommendations:

– Make the achievements of the public administration more visible, enabling subsequent cost-benefit analyses, by: drawing up basic standards for service delivery; monitoring and comparing service demand, *i.e.* workload, staffing levels, costs, quantity, and quality of service provision; encouraging competition between the public and private sectors, among government suppliers, and between administrations themselves; allowing users to judge the service of the public administration.

- Organise the administration as an independent professional body, responsible for administrative management, by: reducing the number of political appointments; separating policy guidance work from ordinary administrative activity; giving more power to independent authorities.
- Consolidate autonomy and the decentralisation of decision-making and managerial powers, by: reviewing legislation on the duties and structures of central government departments; allocating duties on the basis of organic, complementary criteria; giving tax autonomy to regions and local government; no longer earmarking financial transfers; introducing mechanisms to monitor output in autonomous administrations.
- Downscale central government by simplifying government activity, by: reducing the number and scope of central bodies; reducing the various constituent parts in the highest sphere of government; reducing the managerial duties incumbent on the Presidency of the Council of Ministers; periodically reviewing general organisation and specific duties.
- Move from procedure-driven administration to a result-oriented administration, by: simplifying administrative procedures; doing away with intermediate administrative structures; modernising internal communication systems; liberalising private activities.
- Recruit public employees on merit-based criteria and rebuild governance, by: eliminating fixed-term contracts; recruitment based on competitive examination open to everyone; introducing merit- and output-based pay and penalties; increasing the bureaucracy's accountability for ''products''; reducing the number of managers.
- Redistribute resources by cutting down on wastage and enhancing service quality, by: eliminating the invisible cost of corruption; making full use of public assets; periodically monitoring production and results; reforming accounting rules.
- Re-organise administrative premises, by: building new government offices; grouping of offices; extending the number of multi-functional enquiry desks.
- Less but more efficient regulation: lighten the burden of controls, by: drawing up a small set of rules applicable to both public and to private entities.
- Encourage greater integration in the European Union, by: setting up specific offices to deal with relations with the Union; providing European training for public servants.

References

Department of the Public Service (1993), *''La Pubblica Amministrazione nel 1992''*, annual report to Parliament, Rome (Italian text only)

Department of the Public Service (1994), *''Le Aspettative e i Permessi sindacali: Disciplina giuridica e situazione di fatto''*, Rome (Italian text only)

JAPAN

Provisional Council for the Promotion of Administrative Reform (PCPAR)

The Prime Minister requested the PCPAR to examine two issues: "The Role of the Public Sector" and "A Responsive System of Public Administration enabling Policies to be Comprehensive" in September 1992. In response to this request, the PCPAR submitted its "Final Report" to the Prime Minister on 27 October 1993. As a basic principle to reform the administrative system for the 21st century, the final report referred to the following issues:

  $a)$ on "The Role of the Public Sector":
   – sticking to the target ceiling in national debt of a maximum of 50 per cent of GNP;
   – transforming the society from one with bureaucratic leadership to one with autonomy by the people;
   – promoting decentralisation;
  $b)$ on "A Responsive System of Public Administration enabling Policies to be Comprehensive":
   – constructing a comprehensive administrative system;
   – establishing a system to promote further administrative reform.

On 30 October 1993, the PCPAR was dissolved according to its establishment law, after its three-year mission.

Organisational and structural change

The Government strictly examined requests concerning organisations in fiscal year 1993, to prepare a system capable of dealing with diversified demands for public service while controlling overall organisational expansion through rationalisation of the existing structures. For example, the bureaux of the Ministry of Foreign Affairs were re-organised in the interest of more comprehensive and flexible diplomatic policy.

Human resource management: Staff number control

During fiscal year 1993, while implementing the eighth personnel reduction plan which was decided by the Cabinet in July 1991 for the period of FY 1992 to FY 1996 and restricting the addition of new positions, there was a reduction of 1 215 positions. As a result, the total number of national public employees, including both industrial and non-industrial workers, has been reduced by more than 46 000 since the end of FY 1967, which is the base year of the ceiling set by the Total Staff Number Law.

Personnel management reform: Overwork reduction efforts

In order to reduce overtime worked by public servants, it is important for ministries and agencies to co-operate as most overtime work is attributed to interministerial affairs. At the interministerial meeting of personnel management directors, Wednesdays were designated as "No Overwork Days" since January 1993, and it was decided that the government as a whole should make efforts to rationalise interministerial affairs including consultation of drafts of Bills and other policy principles and parliamentary and budgetary affairs. A flexi-time system for research officers was introduced in some government research bodies in April 1993.

Administrative procedures legislation

The Bill of Administrative Procedures Law was submitted to the 126th and 128th sessions of the Diet. While the former died stillborn because of the dissolution of the House of Representatives, the latter was approved and proclaimed in November 1993. Though the law imposes a lot of written rules on the national government (and in part also local governments), including those of procedures for dispositions, the Government is planning to make it effective on 1 October 1994.

The law promotes administrative information disclosure by, for example, requiring agencies to make their criteria known to the public and to show the reason for rejecting applications.

Deregulation

Deregulation came to be regarded as one of the breakthrough measures for the persistent economic depression as well as a tool for the promotion of administrative reform. The Government announced economic measures in April 1993 ("Promotion of Comprehensive Economic Measures") and in September 1993 ("Economic Emergency Measures"). In both policies, deregulation is one of the main elements.

The interim report of the Advisory Group for Economic Structural Reform (the so-called "Hiraiwa Study Group") also focused on deregulation and pointed out its necessity, its principles, supplementary tools for enhancing its effect on the economy, and its perspective.

Decentralisation: Special Scheme for Promoting Decentralisation

Executive outlines of the scheme (introduced in the 1993 Survey) were decided as a consensus between administrative vice-ministers in April 1993. Twenty communities made application (jointly or individually) to the scheme with their original development plan. All the 15 applications were adopted and the first 15 "pilot communities" were designated by the Prime Minister in December 1993.

Privatisation: Offering shares in the East Japan Railway Company

The East Japan Railway Company is one of seven special companies ("*Tokushugaisha*") that took over the business of the former Japan National Railways (JNR), one of the three big public corporations. 62.5 per cent of its shares were offered for public subscription in October 1993. It was the first offer for JNR successors, which had been sought in line with the aim of the JNR reform.

Administrative inspection

During FY 1992, 15 inspection programmes were completed and 17 new inspection programmes were launched. Recommendations were made in areas such as science and technology policy, consumer policy, policy for compulsory schools and management of the Japan Railway Freight Company. During FY 1993, 16 inspection programmes were completed and 19 new inspection programmes were launched. Recommendations were made in areas such as energy policy, policy for students from foreign countries and aviation policy.

LUXEMBOURG

The main purpose of the reform initiatives undertaken in 1993 was to make Luxembourg's public management more efficient, reduce costs and optimise service to the public. There are plans to harmonise the administration using a host of different measures and projects.

Size and structure of the public sector

Since 1 January 1993, the Posts and Telecommunications Administration has become a public enterprise enjoying administrative and financial autonomy and may thus become more competitive. Its staff have retained the status of civil servants.

Another measure adopted by the Council of Ministers on the initiative of the Minister for Finance concerns a reduction in staff costs. Numbers have been cut by freezing one-third of all vacant posts and setting up a system whereby the Commission on Economy and Rationalisation centralises all applications to replace staff leaving the civil service; every month it submits a proposal to the Prime Minister concerning vacant posts that are to remain vacant (one-third), together with vacant posts for re-allocation (two-thirds) to ministries, departments and services that have lost staff. The final decision is taken by the Prime Minister.

Other main fields of public management reform

Several proposed reforms are currently under examination, one being a Bill on the State Personnel Administration. This Administration, originally only a salaries office, has now developed into a full-blown civil service management institution. It deals with the recruitment of many state employees, monitors the enforcement of laws and regulations relating to them, and supervises the introduction of office automation in the public administration. The Government recently decided to put the State Personnel Administration in charge of recruiting replacement staff. It has also been given the task of modernising Luxembourg's civil service with a view to enhancing relations between the administration and its clients.

The Bill is therefore aimed at translating into law the State Personnel Administration's new roles. A number of innovations are introduced:

- A new division is to be set up specifically to handle the replacement of temporarily absent staff.
- The structure of the State Personnel Administration is to be disaggregated, with each division subdivided into sections having their own clearly defined tasks.
- A number of amendments are to be made to civil service pensions, including:
  a) Incorporation into civil service legislation of some private sector provisions concerning survivors' pensions which were introduced under the reform Act of 24 April 1991. This is to ensure social equity and is part of a move launched on 1 January 1988 to improve the harmonisation of the two pension schemes.
  b) The inclusion in civil service pension legislation of a structural improvement in the reversion rate for pensions paid to surviving spouses and orphans in the private sector, but in a form more suited to the civil service pension scheme. Calculated to provide a more advantageous survivors' pension, it is solely for the survivors of civil servants who left the service before completing their career (mainly because of invalidity or death) before the normal retirement age, and who were not entitled to a pension equal to five-sixths of their last salary.
  c) A provision allowing civil servants aged 57 with 40 years' service to apply for early retirement; this entitles them to an old age pension, reduced by 1/60 for every year below the age of 60.

d) When determining entitlement to an old age pension from the age of 60 onward, the acknowledgment of any periods of time spent caring for the aged or the seriously handicapped; these are now deemed to be "auxiliary periods" which count towards 30 years' service.

e) Measures of a more technical nature, which are unrelated to the Act reforming the contribution scheme, but which should amend and supplement legislation on the reform of civil service pensions. These are aimed at resolving problems relating to enforcement and interpretation and at eliminating several loopholes that have arisen in certain areas.

Besides updating pension scheme legislation, the need has arisen to adapt the status of civil servant to the continuously changing world of work. The Bill therefore also deals *inter alia* with the replacement of civil servants on unpaid leave or in part-time employment.

Furthermore, the salary agreement signed in 1990 by the Government and the General Public Service Confederation contains a provision amending the general status of civil servants so as to confer jurisdictional status on the Disciplinary Council. An additional clause will oblige future civil servants to prove sufficient knowledge of the three languages used in the administration.

Finally, the Bill is intended to bring public sector legislation on unpaid leave, following maternity or adoption leave, into line with private sector arrangements.

The main innovations in the Bill in this respect can be summarised as follows:

– If a half-post becomes vacant when a civil servant is given leave to work part-time, another official may be recruited to work part-time on a temporary or permanent basis.
– Job-security is increased for staff on leave.
– The Disciplinary Council, formerly confined to a consultative role, becomes a decision-making body.
– Those applying to join the civil service must now prove sufficient knowledge of the three administrative languages, namely French, German and Luxemburgish.
– Unpaid leave following maternity or adoption leave is extended from one to two years.
– Entitlements due in cases of pregnancy or adoption during unpaid leave or leave to work part-time are amended.
– Civil servants on unpaid leave or leave to work part-time are not allowed to exercise any other lucrative activity in the public or private sector without the prior permission of the Minister for the Public Service.
– In future, any application to resign from the civil service must be made at least two months before the desired date of departure, or may otherwise not be accepted.

NETHERLANDS

Decentralisation: the "normalisation" process

As of 1 April 1993, negotiations on conditions of employment have been decentralised and divided into eight branches: central government, the provinces, municipalities, water control boards, defence, education, the police, and the judiciary. Only pensions, the early retirement scheme (at 61 or after 40 years of service – this is related to developments in the Public Servants Superannuation Fund, ABP) and statutory social security regulations are still to be negotiated centrally for the time being. Decentralising consultations on conditions of employment to the level of the eight branches of the public sector meant that the Minister for Home Affairs is no longer the employer for the entire public service but only for the "central government" branch. For other branches, different ministers have been assigned as the employer, and in some cases collective bodies have been given employers' responsibilities. For example, the Union of Dutch Municipalities assumes the role of employer for the "municipalities" branch.

The responsibilities of the respective employers and the mandates given to them are laid down in a formal protocol. The latter was concluded in February 1993 between the Minister for Home Affairs, the unions, and the representatives of the three lower tiers of government. At the same time, the Minister for Home Affairs reached agreement in principle with the representatives of the unions, to privatise the Public Servants Superannuation Fund (ABP) as of 1 January 1996. The covenant agreed at that time refers not only to the privatisation of the ABP, but also to several matters concerning public sector pensions, the financial framework of the ABP and the Law on Financial Facilities for the Privatisation of the ABP. This Law came into force on 1 May 1994 and settles, *inter alia*, a new system to finance the old age and surviving relative pensions and part of the invalidity pensions.

The above-mentioned privatisation of the ABP entails its establishment as a pension scheme within the meaning of the Pension Funds Guarantee Act (PSW). This Act provides the legal framework for the pension schemes in the private sector. In this way, the role of the government in determining the pension contributions and entitlements of public sector employees will be considerably reduced. At present, the government is responsible for setting the contributions. One of the causes of the financial problems of the ABP was that pension contributions have been set, from the actuarial viewpoint, at an artificially low level for a number of years by means of legislation aimed at withdrawing money from the funds. As of 1 January 1996, this will no longer be the case, because contributions will ultimately be determined by the board of the pension fund constituted under private law. Public sector employers and the representatives of the unions will be represented equally on this board.

As a consequence of the ABP being brought under the PSW, the entitlements of participants in the scheme will no longer be laid down in legislation but in a set of pension provisions. These will be drawn up on the basis of negotiations between employers and employees. At that stage, the normalisation of public sector pensions will be complete.

Integral approach

In April 1993, the Dutch Government decided to increase the cost effectiveness of the public sector as of 1995 by introducing an "integral approach" with respect to the running costs of the public sector. It is assumed that the public sector employers themselves could save 0.7 per cent of salary cost development as a result of their own efficiency measures. The government will in principle not be allowed to set further specific efficiency targets to the budgets for running costs in addition to the 0.7 per cent efficiency increase. An increase in cost effectiveness by public sector employers will have a direct impact on the outcome of the negotiations on conditions of employment in the public sector. It should be mentioned that any improvements in the conditions of employment will be limited if one does not achieve a 0.7 per cent efficiency increase.

Project management freedom versus labour conditions and legal status

In the second half of 1993, an enquiry was undertaken with the aim of making an inventory of the practical problems encountered by managers concerning labour conditions and legal status, both of which can restrict the freedom of managers in fulfilling policy goals. The enquiry produced the result that almost 75% of respondents believe that labour conditions and legal status do not restrict their freedom in fulfilling policy goals. The project group formulated the following suggestions based on the main problems mentioned by respondents. Conditions in the General Civil Service Regulations (ARAR) on temporary jobs and holidays should be deregulated and the possibility of transforming holidays into money should be created. These suggestions will become part of the negotiations with trade unions and ministries.

Senior civil servants

A management development policy extending across all ministries will be established for the approximately 2 000 senior-level national government employees. The Ministry of Home Affairs is also considering setting up an interdepartmental job rotation scheme. Furthermore, an "intertop" database of vacancies of "top jobs" is being built up. It is used to facilitate the exchange of top civil servants throughout the central government. The civil service will gradually be transformed into a general administrative service to enable the government to maintain a qualified and flexible executive staff.

Reform of advisory councils

In 1993, a major reform of the entire structure of advisory boards for the central government was initiated. Following the recommendations of a parliamentary committee, the government started a project aimed at a considerable reduction of the number of advisory councils. The remaining councils will have to deal more with major policy lines and less with details. The advisory system will at the same time be separated from the system of consultancy, where the government discusses its policy initiatives with representatives of economic and social interest groups. All existing advisory councils will be abolished in 1997 (excepting the Council of State). At the same time, a number of new advisory councils will be established and activated. Parliament will be informed several times a year about the progress of the project. A steering committee consisting of top managers from different ministries is in charge of this project.

General Administrative Law

The Dutch Government is at present engaged in a major legislative effort to codify the general part of administrative law. The first two stages of the resulting General Administrative Law Act came into effect on 1 January 1994. The first stage contains provisions on dealings between individuals and administrative authorities, provisions on the application, preparation, publication *etc.* of public orders and provisions on objections and appeals against public orders. The second stage involves the institution of administrative sections of the ordinary courts of first instance, the transfer of most administrative cases to these sections and a uniform Code of Procedure, to be used by both the new administrative sections and the remaining separate administrative courts. Neither the codification of the general part of administrative law nor the reorganisation of the judiciary is completed. Legislation for further stages including rules on subsidies and administrative penalties, is now being prepared.

NEW ZEALAND

1993 was a relatively quiet year for public sector reform in New Zealand. The year was marked by further developments in the capacities of public service organisations to specify the goods and services (outputs) provided to government, and by further enhancements of financial management systems.

There was considerable interest throughout the year about the likely outcome of the General Election which was held in November 1993. The Election was accompanied by a binding referendum on the electoral system (a choice between the existing first-past-the-post system, FPP, and a mixed member proportional system, MMP). The Election returned the National government with a very small majority, while the referendum gave MMP a moderate but still decisive majority. The implications for public sector management and reform will need to be studied over the next year or so.

1993 was a year of consolidation in public sector reform in New Zealand. Reform initiatives from previous years progressed, in particular concerning changes to the management of the health sector.

Size and structure of the public sector

Limits to the size of the public sector

There were no major initiatives introduced that were intended to reduce the size or scope of the public sector. Initiatives that were completed did, however, continue to reduce the size of the core public service. Notable areas of change were in transport, where services were moved to a number of Crown entities (Aviation Security Service, Land Transport Safety Authority, Maritime Safety Authority, Civil Aviation Authority). These are non-departmental separate agencies run by boards which have been given responsibility for the Government's involvement in the various transport sectors. The now very much smaller Ministry of Transport remains in the core public service as a policy agency.

Privatisation

During the year, New Zealand Rail, the State-owned enterprise that owned and operated the country's rail network and inter-island ferry service, was sold. A number of local electricity supply authorities were privatised during the year. These authorities, which had belonged to local authorities, were privatised generally through a process of share issues involving some distribution of shares to the community.

Decentralisation within central government

The major area of reform in this field continued to be in the management of the New Zealand health system. Four regional health authorities (RHAs) are now fully established to act as funding bodies for the provision of health services to the community. Providers of health services contract with RHAs. Publicly-owned providers (Crown health enterprises or CHEs) are required to seek funding in a market-driven environment.

Use of market-type mechanisms

The objectives of the health reforms are to seek to introduce market disciplines into the health system in order to generate efficiency gains and to set and maintain appropriate standards of health care.

New roles for central management bodies

Since the major changes to the roles of the three central agencies (the Department of the Prime Minister and Cabinet, the State Services Commission, and the Treasury) that were brought about by the introduction of the State Sector Act 1988 and the Public Finance Act 1989, there has been little further change. Both the Treasury and the State Services Commission have continued to adapt their structures and resourcing to the new operating environment.

Other main fields of public management reform

Management of policy-making

Efforts are being made to improve the co-ordination of policy advice provided by core public service departments to the Government. This is being done through developing processes and protocols to ensure that departments consult with each other during the preparation of individual policy papers, and also through the mechanisms being developed to focus departments in support of strategic objectives articulated by the Government.

During the year, the Government developed and produced a document setting out its objectives for the country (*The Path to 2010*). This document was intended to outline the Government's broad strategic objectives for New Zealand.

Clear specification at the departmental level is obviously most effective where the strategic goals of Government are themselves clearly defined. A significant step towards this was taken with the examination of the relationship of chief executive performance agreements to the Government's strategic objectives.

Performance management

A central theme underlying the reform programme has been decentralisation of decision-making in return for appropriate levels of accountability and responsibility. The key mechanism for articulating this relationship has been the chief executive performance agreement. The chief executive is in a very formal way the key link between Government strategy and departmental action.

In 1993, departmental chief executive performance agreements were modified to set out the requirements in three parts:
– Part I relates to the personal performance of individual chief executives. Its content – which should encapsulate the strategic objectives and specific priority tasks that the minister and chief executive agree are the key result areas – is a matter for discussion and agreement between the minister and the chief executive.
– Part II of the performance agreement covers the Government's purchase interest in the department (now specified in the newly required purchase agreement between minister and chief executive).
– Part III of the performance agreement covers the Government's ownership interests, including a number of legislative requirements (for example, the good employer and equal employment opportunities obligations of the State Sector Act and the financial management and reporting requirements of the Public Finance Act) as well as specific Cabinet directives in support of the collective interests of Government (for example, payfixing, senior management development, property management, energy management, and information management obligations).

Financial resources management

The Treasury has primary responsibility for this area of public sector management. As reported in the 1993 Survey, all Crown-owned entities are now required to operate within uniform and consistent accountability and financial reporting structures.

The budget process has benefited significantly in recent years from the incorporation of a three-year focus. The Government has already signalled its intention to strengthen this focus and to create a more useful set of estimates for Parliament, ministers, and departments.

Personnel management

Responsibility for personnel management in the public service has been largely devolved to individual departments. The State Services Commission continues to be involved with departmental chief executives to develop systems for senior management development, guidelines for appropriate managerial practices, and codes of ethics for public servants.

NORWAY

Size and structure of the public sector

Limits to the size of the public sector

The Government presented the report on the **Long-term Programme 1994-97** (Report No. 4 to the *Storting* (1992-93) Long-term Programme 1994-97). The main tasks outlined in the programme are to set the stage for a lasting improvement in employment and an increase in value added to solve the welfare tasks. A central theme of the programme is therefore the long-term development of trade and industry. At the same time, production and consumption must be kept within the limits set by the natural environment.

To ensure room for an active use of the government budget also in the future, the Long-term Programme states that the growth of public expenditure should not exceed the growth of the economy as a whole during the programme period. In the preparation of the programme, the Government has taken as a basis that the underlying growth of central government expenditure during the programme period as a whole should not exceed GNP growth for mainland Norway. The Government's reform proposals will to a large extent be covered by corresponding savings elsewhere in the budget.

The Government also states in the Long-term Programme that a strong public sector constitutes an important element of future welfare society. The public sector should be structured with a view to "contributing to enhanced quality of life for the individual and increased efficiency in the economy at large". The use of resources in the public sector will be re-assessed on a continuing basis in order to achieve the best possible results from given inputs.

Due to technological changes, increased competition, internationalisation, new challenges, budgetary pressures, etc., a number of central government agencies will be forced to reduce their staff over the next few years. This is in particular the case for the large public enterprises within the communications sector (the **Postal Service**, the **Telecommunications Service** and the **Railways Service**) and the **defence services**. On the other hand, some agencies are expanding their staff due to changing priorities and needs, *i.e.* the police and prison services, the employment service and universities and colleges.

It is general government policy to avoid dismissals in connection with these readjustment efforts. So far, most agencies have been able to handle changing personnel needs through training measures, internal redeployment, early retirement and other efforts to stimulate employees to leave voluntarily. In the Telecommunications Service and the Railways Service, surplus personnel have been transferred to separate units offering training, etc.

As reported in the 1993 Survey, a **Redeployment and Readjustment Unit** was established in the Ministry of Government Administration in 1993. The unit shall assist ministries and agencies readjusting their personnel needs to new demands and shall, among other things, try to increase mobility between different parts of the civil service.

Commercialisation or corporatisation of public bodies

The **Civil Aviation Authority** and the **Government Construction and Properties Agency** were turned into public enterprises from 1993. From 1994, the **Norwegian Geographical Survey** and the **Norwegian Guarantee Institute for Export Credits** will be turned into public enterprises.

An evaluation of the organisational status of the **Postal Service**, the **Telecommunications Service** and the **Railways Service** was started in 1993. The main alternatives for each agency are to continue as a public enterprise or to be given corporate status, either as a State-owned enterprise or as a State-owned limited stock company.

Decentralisation to sub-national government

The responsibility for the **local offices of the agricultural and forestry service** will be transferred to the municipalities from 1 January 1994. From 1 July 1993, the County Agricultural and Forestry Offices were turned into new **Departments of Agriculture and Forestry** of the county governor. The 18 county governors are the principal representatives of central government at the local level.

Deconcentration within central government

The central government **health administration** was re-organised on 1 January 1994 the Directorate of Health becoming the Board of Health. As a part of the re-organisation, a number of tasks will be delegated from the central level to the chief county medical officers. The chief county medical officer is the central government health administration's principal representative at the local level.

Other restructuring or "rationalisation" efforts

A committee to consider the organisation of the **tax and excise administration** presented its report in 1993. A majority of the committee members recommends that the various agencies within this sector (the Directorate of Taxes, the Directorate of Customs and Excise and the Tax Collectors) should be re-organised into one combined agency. This proposition has now been presented to the *Storting*.

Other main fields of public management reform

Management of policy-making

As a consequence of Norway's entry into the European Economic Area (EEA), the Norwegian government has adopted a **decision-making structure for the central government administration's handling of EEA-related matters**. Important aspects of the system are to ensure that Norway speaks with a single and co-ordinated voice, that decisions are made in a swift and efficient way, and that EEA issues are well integrated into the ordinary work of ministries and agencies.

Performance management

The programme to introduce **performance management in the budgetary process** continued in 1993 with the work on the 1994 budget. The experience so far shows that this process will take some time. However, all ministries are now in the process of developing performance measures/indicators, setting performance targets and publishing these in the budget proposition to Parliament. A project on improving the ministries' letters of allocation to their subordinate agencies based on performance management principles has been started. Priority areas for 1994 are to improve reporting systems and to develop ministerial management of external agencies.

The Ministry of Government Administration has issued guidelines on **the use of executive committees in the central government administration**. The guidelines will help ministries when considering whether an executive committee might be an appropriate instrument with which to manage a government service for which they are responsible. As a general principle, the guidelines state that a central government agency should not normally have an executive committee. However, in certain cases, and provided the agency's assignments do not involve the exercise of authority or the formulation of policy, conditions may exist for the appropriate use of executive committees. When executive committees are used, they should be given extensive powers.

Financial resources management

The Ministry of Finance has issued a circular on the use of rules of exemption in the **Budgetary Regulations**. Following the many changes in the budgetary system since 1985, the Ministry of Finance has made a number of decisions on the use of rules of exemption over the years, which have been published in separate circulars. The new circular gives updated and complete information on the use of rules of exemption as well as defining the line ministries' responsibility for ensuring that central government agencies are able to benefit from and to utilize the budgetary reforms.

Personnel management

The Ministry of Government Administration has started a comprehensive assessment of the two **civil service pay systems** introduced in 1991: a new "main" system covering most of the civil servants, and a new performance-related pay system for top managers.

The Ministry of Government Administration has drawn up a "**Strategy for Management Development** in the Central Government Sector in 1993-95". The strategy includes guidelines for both the central management and the operational level. The line ministries are, however, responsible for management development within the agencies under their responsibility.

The Ministry of Government Administration has drawn up a **strategy for general personnel development** for civil servants. The agencies are responsible for developing their own employees. The Ministry of Government Administration will, however, continue to offer guidance and also centrally organised training courses in areas of strategic importance.

In 1993, the work on improving the sets of rules and regulations concerning pay and personnel has been concentrated on the reduction of the so-called "**special agreements**", which are agreements between the various ministries, agencies and institutions and the civil service unions.

An **employers' association** for government-owned enterprises, companies, *etc.*, was established at the end of 1993.

Regulatory management and reform

The Ministry of Government Administration has prepared a draft **checklist on the assessment of new regulations**. The draft checklist has been presented to ministries and other institutions for comments. The Ministry plans to publish the checklist in its "guidelines series" in the Spring of 1994.

Improving relations with citizens/enterprises

A trial project on **public administration service offices ("one-stop shops")** has been started. The service offices will integrate the field services of various central government and local government agencies. In1993, three offices were established. A further five will be opened in1994.

Management of information technology

The **Sector Plan for IT in Public Administration** has been followed up with a number of projects and activities in1993. The Ministry of Government Administration has presented draft guidelines on information resources management. The draft guidelines have been presented to relevant institutions for comments. Within the standardisation field, NOSIP (Norwegian OSI-profile for use in both public administration and private industry) and NORBÅS (framework for the use of open systems solutions in public administration) have been finished. A number of projects have been started in the fields of information exchange between central and local government and public administration information gathering from the private sector.

Other

The Ministry of Government Administration and the Ministry of Local Government and Labour have presented draft guidelines on **central government agencies' inspection and control of private industry**. An important aspect of the guidelines is to improve the co-ordination and coherence between the various agencies as far as inspection practices are concerned.

PORTUGAL

The evolution of public management in Portugal in 1993 followed the guidelines laid down in the "Major Options Plan", which were as follows:

- **quality:** developing and carrying out programmes to encourage quality in public services;
- **rationalisation:** increasing effectiveness of human and financial resources;
- **bringing the administration closer to the citizen:** keeping citizens informed as to services available and standards required;
- **qualification:** improving and motivating civil servants' skills in the carrying out of their duties;
- **privatisation:** making openings for the private sector by channelling financial resources to those sectors of the public service which need reinforcement in the carrying out of their duties to the public, and withdrawing from areas of activity where market and competitive norms are applicable.

Based on these objectives, the following initiatives should be highlighted.

Quality

The **"Public Service Quality Charter"** was drawn up and contains the general principles and recommendations for drafting sectoral quality charters which, in turn, should state clearly and objectively the commitments required between services and clients.

In the ambit of activities to make better known the "Public Service Quality Charter", a conference on administrative modernisation, **"Quality in Public Services: Commitment to the Citizen"**, was organised in co-operation with the Public Management Service of the OECD.

The first **"Quality in Public Services Awards"** were promoted and prizes were presented to the award-winning services by the Prime Minister on the National Day for Debureaucratisation.

Raising the standards of public services was the common denominator in the analysis and recommendations made by the Commission for Quality and Rationalisation of the Public Administration, which published its report **"Renovating the Public Administration: a Challenge and Commitment"**.

The collecting of used paper and the use of recycled paper is being encouraged in the public services.

The convergence of the quality policy in public administration with the national policy for quality was actively promoted.

Rationalisation

An **evaluation study on the impact of information technology** on the public administration was made based on an enquiry made through the central administration, which was discussed and assessed at a meeting of top managers organised in conjunction with the Public Management Service.

The Reform of Public Accounting and the Treasury was carried through, namely by the implementation in 12 departments of the Finance Ministry of an instrumental module for financial management (SIC); a central accounting system (SSC); a public data transmission network; and the introduction of alternative Treasury payment methods (MPT) which utilize the electronic transfer of funds via the electronic banking network SIBS (Interbanking Services Company).

The **legislative re-organisation** of various government departments has almost been completed.

The **rationalisation of administrative structures** and **management flexibility** were also dealt with by the Commission for Quality and Rationalisation of the Public Administration.

Bringing the administration closer to the citizen

The highlight was the setting up and inauguration of five user-friendly, multi-media, computerised kiosks, INFOCID ("Interdepartmental System for Citizens' Information"). These kiosks have been set up to provide clear, precise, up-to-date information on procedures, rights and duties of citizens and the public administration, as well as organisation and location of services.

A **Public Services Guide** was compiled and made available in printed and magnetic form.

The Commission for Enterprise/Administration relationships (CEA) has set up a one-stop public notary (a notary empowered to speed up and facilitate all legal measures required for the incorporation of companies).

Debureaucratisation measures were also put into practice:

- the publication of "One Thousand Administrative Measures" has brought public attention to a variety of measures which have been implemented in the areas of simplification of procedures and receptiveness to clients;
- the removal of the necessity for a notarial deed to effect the transfer of real property intended for habitation, and which in the future can be effected by private instrument;
- alterations to the Commercial Registry Code, simplifying registration procedures and enabling photocopies to be requested verbally;
- revising the Portuguese classification of economic businesses, thereby completing industrial activity regulations.

Qualification

The Government approved the **"Public Service Deontological Charter"** containing the fundamental values of public service and the duties of public servants towards citizens, the public administration, sovereign bodies, the organs of the governments of the autonomous regions, and the organs of local authorities. A seminar to discuss and promote the "Public Service Deontological Charter", which was distributed throughout the public services, was held in collaboration with the Public Management Service.

PROFAP ("Integrated Programme for Training in Public Administration Modernisation") is being carried out with financial aid from both the European Social Fund and the European Regional Development Fund. In the ambit of the programme, 3 021 training initiatives have been carried out, which involved 53 084 participants and totalled 2 433 828 training hours. Preparatory work for PROFAP II (1994-99) is already being carried out. This programme will be integrated into the new Community Support Plan (QCA).

The basic law for professional training in public administration has been approved, containing namely a clarification of the role of central and sectoral bodies in this connection, the creation of consultative bodies with trade union participation, and the definition of the system for the recognition of training institutions.

Privatisation

The policy to privatise nationalised and government administrated companies continues to be carried out and has given rise to the adoption of a number of market-type mechanisms. In this ambit, special reference must be made to the work and report of the Commission for Quality and Rationalisation of the Public Administration. One of the principal objectives of the report is to promote and stimulate debate on responsibilities assumed by the State and also to encourage withdrawal of the State in those areas where the market sector provides cost-effective quality services which observe the rights of consumers.

Other

Finally, reference must also be made to the fact that work has begun on a "case study" on public management reform strategies developed and implemented during the last two decades. This is being undertaken in collaboration with the Public Management Service.

SPAIN

Size and structure of the public sector

Limiting the present size of the public sector

The present size of the public sector in Spain can be determined by two major measures: first public expenditure as a proportion of GDP, and second employment. With respect to expenditure, between 1982 and 1992, public expenditure rose from 38.2 per cent to 45.1 per cent. This steep increase brought Spain 6.5 points closer to the average of other countries in the European Union, although it was still 4.1 points behind that average.

The economic policy measures adopted in 1993 were aimed at reducing the public deficit by reining in public expenditure in the public administration as a whole. The strategy used to achieve this was to curb salary increases for public employees and to freeze recruitment by not issuing public service vacancy notices.

The 1993 General State Budgets Act awarded an increase in public sector salaries that was, for the first time, lower than the cost-of-living index. A 10 per cent reduction was also made in vacant posts under the Council of Ministers agreement of July 1992.

With respect to the second measure (employment), the policy is to optimise existing human resources, by freezing recruitment from the outside. The legislative measures on the public service recently approved by Parliament aim at rationalising and restructuring administrative bodies. This is the principle behind Employment Plans, part of a comprehensive human resource strategy for the various administrative bodies now trying to match their internal labour market to real needs with a view to increasing efficiency.

The move to freeze recruitment will end the steady upward trend in staffing levels which brought in 533 636 new staff. This figure still leaves Spain three percentage points behind other EU countries when compared with the labour force as a whole (EU average 17.41 per cent, average for Spain 14.5 per cent).

The steepest increase between 1982 and 1993 occurred in the Autonomous Communities (562 834 people), followed by local government (almost 200 000), university administration (over 40 000) and legal administration (over 19 000). The number of central government staff, which in 1982 accounted for 77.59 per cent of all public administration personnel, fell by almost 300 000 during this time as a result of transfers to the Autonomous Communities. Once the transfer of central government staff is completed under the recent Transfer Act, the Autonomous Communities will have twice as many staff as central government.

Public institutions: experiments with commercialisation or corporatisation of public bodies

The 1992 EU Convergence Plan provides for economic liberalisation in some sectors with monopolies, such as telecommunications and oil distribution, as well as international road transport. The Plan also provides for private sector participation in certain public sector activities, a reduction in the number of public bodies, and a freeze, in nominal terms, in subsidies to public enterprises.

Another objective is to run certain public services as closely as possible along private sector lines. This was the aim behind major changes, within the state administration, concerning the legal regime governing the provision of essential services, namely tax management, postal services, ports and airports. These public services are in fact based on private sector law to achieve greater resource efficiency and cost-effectiveness. However, the lack of an appropriate legal framework for the creation of public institutions to be run along commercial lines made it impossible, in 1993, to establish new public bodies.

In addition, in 1993 a Data Protection Agency was established, as an independent body responsible for checking that the Act on the processing of personal computer data is properly applied.

The Ministry for Public Administration (MAP) is currently working on a project concerning the Act on the organisation and operation of central government services and their subordinate bodies. This will establish the appropriate prescriptive framework for new public bodies to be set up, and will strike a balance between managerial autonomy and government monitoring of results.

Decentralisation to other levels of government

The extent to which the three levels of government in Spain – central, Autonomous Communities and local – are decentralised is based on the structure of public expenditure, *i.e.* the share in that expenditure of each level of government. During the period 1982-93, considerable progress was made in the decentralisation of central government to the Autonomous Communities. Consequently, these Communities now account for a greater share of public expenditure as a whole, moving from 6.1 per cent in 1982 to 24.3 per cent in 1993. Over the same period, local government also saw its share rise from 9.5 per cent to 14.5 per cent. Central government, on the other hand, registered a decrease of 23 percentage points, falling from 84.7 per cent in 1982 to 61.2 per cent in 1993.

The decentralisation of public expenditure over the next few years will involve more major changes to the benefit of both local government and the Autonomous Communities, given the new responsibilities that those Communities with the least authority should now take up. The first moves to extend powers date from 1993 under the "Act transferring powers to the Autonomous Communities, which acquired autonomy under Article 143 of the Constitution". An organic Act, it provides for 32 new transfers of responsibility to the Autonomous Communities, involving budgets of over Ptas 1 billion, and gives each Community virtually the same level of responsibility, except with respect to healthcare management in the social security system.

Ultimately, as local government takes on greater powers, there will be a shift in public expenditure, giving a breakdown of 50 per cent for central government, 25 per cent for the Autonomous Communities and 25 per cent for local government. Furthermore, in the course of 1993 major progress was made on sharing fiscal responsibility with the Autonomous Communities, based on new formulae for distributing central government taxation revenue.

New role for central management bodies

1993 marked the introduction of the evaluation mechanisms provided for in the Council of Ministers agreement of April 1992, which approved a Modernisation Plan comprising over 200 projects affecting all ministries for implementation in 1992/93. Sixty of the projects are concerned with improving government information and communication between the citizen and the administration, 80 with enhancing the quality of services directly impacting upon the citizen, and 64 with internal management, as a necessary means to the ends of either providing better quality services or managing the available resources more efficiently.

For approved projects, the Plan provides for result assessments at two levels. In all cases, the minister responsible is required to conduct an internal evaluation. The second evaluation is carried out by two ministries with horizontal responsibilities over the administration as a whole (Ministry of Finance, and Ministry for Public Administration), by means of two new monitoring and appraisal bodies, one chaired by the Minister for Public Administration and the other by the Vice-President of the Government.

Personnel management policies are developed, planned and evaluated by the Directorates-General for Public Administration and Organisation, Establishment Posts and Informatics in the Ministry for Public Administration and by the Directorate-General for Staff Costs at the Ministry of Finance.

Finally the recent Act, approved by Parliament in December 1993, partially amending the legal regime for the public service, gives important powers to both horizontal ministries in two areas, namely approving the Employment Plans drawn up by each ministerial department and, in the absence of any proposal from the department concerned, taking the initiative in drawing up such a plan.

Employment Plans, as has already been said, can be one way of fully implementing the policies an administrative body should use to optimise its available human resources. The powers conferred upon the horizontal ministries by this Act underline the importance attached to the duties of development, planning and outcome evaluation incumbent upon central management bodies.

Public management reforms: leading aspects

Personnel management

In 1993, the management/union Agreement was implemented to improve working conditions and a substantial amount of analysis and applied research was carried out in the field of staff planning, focusing on administrative career development, retirement conditions, performance appraisal, etc.

A manual on human resource management has streamlined management procedures.

Further decentralisation of authority from central to sectoral management bodies is taking place.

A specific policy for senior and middle management has drawn upon training plans and improved recruitment using a database on the profiles and career paths of senior and middle managers.

More Spanish public servants have been taking part in European Union programmes, in particular "Karolus" (Action Plan for the exchange of national officials who are engaged in the implementation of Community legislation required to achieve the internal market).

The legal regime governing the public service has gained in flexibility following the recent approval of a law changing several of its aspects. In 1994, there are plans to draw up and approve Employment Plans for each ministerial department, thereby adapting the internal labour market to the true needs of each body.

The prescriptive changes introduced under the new Act make it possible to initiate a staff redeployment policy, which involves finding sectors or sections of government with too many or too few staff and transferring human resources from one to the other.

Additional measures which have been introduced, include voluntary leave of absence with benefits, early retirement with benefits, early retirement and phased-out termination of employment.

Improving citizen-administration relations

Better relations between citizens and the administration is one of the objectives of the Council of Ministers Agreement signed in April 1992. As a result of the Agreement, 200 practical projects have received approval, 60 of them aimed at improving information and communication between citizens and the administration.

One project set up in 1993 involves the identification of civil service staff. Its aim is to make officials more responsive by enabling the public to know who it is that they are dealing with. Different staff/citizen relationships are defined, appropriate forms of identification are established for each, and they are incorporated into an identification system covering all public employees.

As a further part of the strategy to improve public access to the administration, the following measures have been introduced:

– more enquiry desks in ministerial departments and public bodies;
– a new telephone service to answer users' questions, located in the MAP's Administrative Information Centre. The purpose of the service is to provide people with basic information so as to avoid unnecessary visits, and to inform people where the relevant management units are situated.

SWEDEN

Reforming public administration

The present Government's accession to power in Autumn 1991 involved a break with the traditional "Swedish model" in favour of a more market-oriented economic policy. The Government set itself four major tasks, which were to dominate its endeavours during the mandate period, namely:

- restoring Sweden as a nation of growth and enterprise;
- improving social welfare through revolutionary freedom of choice;
- leading Sweden into European co-operation; and
- shaping a long-term and sustainable trend towards a society characterised by a healthy environment.

Current changes in public administration are aimed at creating instruments for, and promoting the realisation of, the general objectives adopted by the *Riksdag* (Swedish Parliament) and Government. Individuals and families are to be given greater room for manœuvre at the expense of rigidified bureaucratic regulations and public sector monopolies. The State's commitments in various sectors of society must be clearly and unequivocally defined. Alternatives and diversity are to be stimulated in health and social care, and other public services to citizens. Quasi-market conditions are to be introduced in public sector production for the purpose of attaining efficient resource allocation.

The reassessment and renewal of the various systems and institutions of the public sector that took place in 1993 formed part of this policy. The following major initiatives were undertaken during 1993.

Size and structure of the public sector

Limits to the size of the public sector

In pursuit of balance and stability in public finances, the *Riksdag* resolved in Spring 1993 on a programme to put public finances on a sound basis. This includes a curb on public consumption in order to keep expenditure unchanged in real terms. As a result of the structural changes in public administration, the number of State employees fell by some 48 000 between September 1992 and September 1993.

Privatisation

The Government launched its privatisation programme in December 1991, empowered by the *Riksdag* to sell shares in 34 wholly or partially State-owned companies, with the intention of exposing them to market forces and competition. During 1993, a number of privatisation measures were carried out. All State-owned shares in *Celsius Industrier AB*, the defence industry group, were sold to the public, employees and foreign institutions. Privatisation also took place in the markets for computer services, venture capital and investments.

Privatisation is also occurring through the State's transfer of certain portions of its activities to pre-existing private companies. Examples of this are the Swedish Armed Forces' Computer and Media Centres.

In December 1993, the Government announced that in Spring 1994 it would offer shares in the forest industry group *AssiDomän AB* and the pharmaceutical company *Pharmacia* for broad-based sale on the market. For *AssiDomän AB*, the aim is to get the company quoted on the stock exchange.

Private alternatives are being promoted in sectors where central and local government activities are unsuitable for total privatisation. In the education sector, equivalent terms have been introduced for free-standing schools, and individuals have been given a statutory right to a personal choice of school. The family doctor reform in the health care sector makes greater accessibility and continuity possible. In child care, the local authorities are being obliged to pay grants for private alternatives as well. The introduction of child care grants for parents, too, will help to foster the emergence of private alternatives.

Commercialisation of public bodies

Efforts to turn State enterprises into limited companies have continued. In 1993, Swedish Telecom became *Telia AB*. In December 1993, the *Riksdag* resolved that Sweden Post would be incorporated. State testing and research activities and property acquisition have also been entrusted to limited companies; the same applies to State vaccine production, in preparation for privatisation.

Decentralisation of sub-national government

In 1993, a new system of government grants to local authorities was introduced. The chief purpose of the new grants is to put the local authorities on an equal financial footing. This is to be attained by evening out their economic disparities and giving them all possible freedom to shape their own activities. In conjunction with this, numerous earmarked government grants have been discontinued, along with the detailed control regulations associated with these grants.

The new system of government grants was devised in an attempt to decentralise public sector functions and enhance the local authorities' autonomy. Another reason is to bring about a clearer division of responsibility between the central and local government sectors. The State now governs by pursuing over-riding aims, and its monitoring of local government is concentrated on the fulfilment of these aims.

Use of quasi-market mechanisms

Public sector production is being reduced to essentials. These should be the cores sectors of central and local government, *i.e.* activities that cannot be conducted on market terms alone and should therefore not be incorporated; these include education and health care. Continuous reviews are carried out for the purpose of exposing to competition activities conducted under public auspices. Quasi-market conditions for such activities are obtained by, for example, introducing the customer-executor model.

In November 1993, the board of the Swedish Association of Local Authorities adopted an action programme to intensify competition for tenders in the local government sector, as a means of raising efficiency and quality alike. The Swedish Agency for Administrative Development and the National Competition Board were charged with studying how far the State and local authorities procure services and products through competitions for tenders.

New role for central administrative bodies

The Swedish Agency for Administrative Development has been given a clearer and more focused role as the staff organisation for the Government, Cabinet Office and ministries. The Agency formerly also served as a consultative body for government agencies. This sometimes resulted in contradictions between its two roles. Linking the Agency more closely to the Cabinet Office and ministries is one aspect of the skills and resource allocation necessitated by the work of reforming public administration. The Agency is to provide documentation for the Government's review, rationalisation and control.

As for the National Agency of Government Employers (SAV), a major organisational reform was passed by the *Riksdag* in 1993. The aim is to make SAV more independent from the Government and, as far as possible, place it on the same footing as the employers' confederation in the private sector. SAV is now to be financed not by grants under the national budget, but by charges levied on the agencies. The agencies will gain more influence over the main activities, such as collective bargaining and policy issues common to employers.

This reform is closely connected with the new budget principle whereby, in brief, the Government is to impose the agencies' overall financial limits each year – limits that may not be exceeded. The system of adjusting grant figures afterwards according to the central collective agreements between SAV and the trade unions has been abandoned. Accordingly, these agreements no longer require government approval.

Minor adjustments regarding Government control, as laid down in the Constitution, are currently under way.

Other main fields of public administration reforms

Performance management

The Government's aim has been to restructure public administration in order to make it more efficient and flexible. One important element in this work has been a modification of the budget process.

The need for long-term and more in-depth analysis of activities and a transition to performance management was what underlay the budget reform. The work of reform was initiated in 1988, stepped up in 1992 and maintained in 1993. The in-depth accounting and scrutiny of the entire field of activity for which the agency concerned is responsible, which used to take place once every three years, have been developed and made more flexible. The Cabinet Office and ministries now decide, on the basis of what the activity requires, on the dates when in-depth examination is to be undertaken. An in-depth examination of this kind results in a planning framework with a long-term perspective for control of activities. The planning framework then provides the guidelines for changing activities over the forthcoming budget period.

Positive effects of the new budget process have already been observed:

- Agencies are engaged in assessing their own work and its future orientation – not only in their financial departments, but throughout the organisation.
- Annual reports received by the Government have been better in relation to the documentation for decision-making available previously. Information has shown in a clearer way what has been achieved and what can be corrected. This is an improvement for both the Government and the agency itself.

In the future development of the budget process, the requirements for performance management will be clarified and those for reporting financial results defined more precisely. There will be a clearer focus than hitherto on analysing results as part of the agency's more detailed grant application.

Financial resource management

In consequence of the modification of the budget process, the budget principles have also been changed. The underlying purpose may be summarised as follows:

- The agencies' activities are to be assessed as a whole, and the size of the grant is an expression of the level of ambitions decided upon and expected in these activities.
- The general price trend in the sector in question should constitute the starting point for compensation for cost trends for all types of resource.
- The Government's responsibility within the framework of the national budget process should be clearly distinguished from matters incumbent on the State as an employer.

Concentration of forms of activity in public administration continued in 1993. Activities exposed to competition are considered unsuitable for being conducted in public agency form. An appropriate form of activity for these is, instead, a limited company or a foundation.

Financial control is aimed at achieving more efficient systems of State management of funds at "corporate-group level" and also greater scope for delegating financial powers to the agencies. The introduction of an interest-bearing account for the agencies' grant payments and also market loans from the National Debt Office to finance investments in fixed assets are aimed at enhancing the agencies' cost awareness.

As a result of the performance-oriented control of agencies and the delegated financial powers, incentives are created for the agencies to handle their own resources efficiently. The purpose of this technique is to define the agencies' room for manœuvre more clearly in advance. Requirements imposed on the agencies are clarified so that, at an early stage, they know the financial limits of their activities and how they will be compensated for cost trends. Within these limits, the agencies are given extensive financial freedom. Internal decisions within the scope of activities, such as local influence on pay determination, are one example of this.

Personnel management

Development of State personnel policy has been governed by the renewal programme for the public sector that was initiated in the mid-1980s. Central control can no longer function efficiently in a society characterised by diversity, mobility, change and internationalisation. Far-reaching delegation of powers from the Government to agencies has taken place. The individual agencies have gained such influence over pay determination, etc., that they have been able to adapt personnel policy to their own requirements and needs. The agencies decide for themselves what form of work organisation, what personnel strength and what skills they should have in order best to attain the defined objectives within their financial limits.

A substantial deregulation has also taken place in order, as far as possible, to harmonise public service employees' personnel policy terms with the regulations applying to the rest of the labour market.

Given the new budget process and far-reaching delegation, the Government sees its dialogue with the agency heads as a highly important instrument of control. How far the agency directors succeed in their leadership is crucially important for how the *Riksdag's* and Government's aim of boosting efficiency in the central government sector is fulfilled. Very heavy responsibility is therefore borne by the agency director. To guarantee an ample supply of directors, the Ministry of Finance is engaged in a large-scale programme of skills development, including introductory seminars, follow-up career discussions and seminars on topical issues. The work of professional recruitment and managerial development will be intensified.

Regulatory management and reform

Under the designation "Quality of regulations", wide-ranging efforts are under way to review regulations and effect deregulation. One purpose of this deregulation is to open up public markets to competition. A special delegation has been charged with compiling and specifying regulation amendments and other measures to increase competition and growth. These efforts are under way in all the departments and ministries, in a deregulation programme. Among the sectors currently due for deregulation are education and housing.

Improving relations with citizens and enterprises

The new public administration that is emerging involves a clearer distinction between central and local government activities. The local authorities themselves may shape their own activities. To make matters easier for private citizens, "citizens' bureaux" have been set up on an experimental basis. These bureaux collect all public services offered by central and local government under one roof.

Management of information technology

As part of the delegation of State powers in progress, the agencies are now no longer obliged to obtain approval for their procurement and use of information technology. Investments in information technology are financed by the agency through market loans.

Internationalisation

Augmented European co-operation plays an ever more prominent role in Swedish public administration. Greater knowledge will be required. Although retaining the basic structure of Swedish public administration is expected to be feasible, substantial organisational changes will probably be necessary.

The Government has had the organisation of the European Union in various official sectors surveyed and, in so doing, investigated issues relating to Sweden's possible participation in EU co-operation. In 1993, for the purpose of preparation, all the departments, ministries and respective agencies concerned investigated how activities in the corresponding administrative areas are organised and conducted in the EU.

SWITZERLAND

The public sector and its recent evolution

In November 1990, the Federal Council charged a group of experts – working closely with a parliamentary committee – with the task of developing new management structures for the Confederation, central government and federal administration. In fact, a reform of the Government implies a reform of the administration, the latter being the vehicle of Government action. The first phase of this reform will be at the legislative level, in the context of the Constitution now in force. The main lines are to relieve the Government of certain administrative tasks, thus allowing it to concentrate on its political responsibilities, and to make management structures more flexible so as to better define the priorities of government action and to make that action more effective. Thus the key themes of this reform are flexibility and deregulation. The range of measures for achieving these goals appeared in the proposal that the Government submitted to Parliament on 20 October 1993. The second phase of the reform will be based on the experience of these first measures, and will concern constitutional matters. In this context, a review will be made of the role of Swiss institutions and of the validity of established political values. No deadline has been set for this second phase.

Monitoring and evaluation of reforms

The measures proposed by the working group on "legislative evaluation" have been made specific and developed. The major elements are the introduction of evaluation as a management tool for heads of department, and training or refresher courses in evaluation techniques. In 1994, the Federal Council will decide on actions to follow-up the recommendations of the working group.

New reforms in 1993

Work to introduce management control in the federal administration continued. Some of the main points were:

- finalisation of the detailed concepts concerning "Global management control for the Energy 2000 programme" (Federal Office of Energy) and "Management control strategy for cereal production" (Federal Office of Agriculture);
- support to those two offices in their preliminary work;
- continued development of the detailed concept "Management control of implementation of the law on investment aid in mountainous regions".

The project "Management control in the federal administration" was presented to approximately 300 public administration managers, at a seminar held respectively in German and in French at both federal and cantonal levels. In addition, two new seminars (in French) – organised in co-operation with the Federal Office of Personnel – were held to present "Management control in the federal administration" to approximately 30 managers in the federal administration. The project itself has been presented directly in 12 offices of the federal administration, in universities in Lausanne and Geneva, and to the Public Management Committee of the OECD.

TURKEY

Size and structure of the public sector

Limits to the size of the public sector

The restructuring and streamlining of the State has been accepted as the basic principle in the Government Programme, and within this context it has been emphasized that there should also be a reduction in the number of personnel. Consequently, the Prime Ministry has decided not to create new positions that would cause an expansion of organisations and paralyse financial saving measures. The requirement for new posts should be met by changing the classifications, titles and grades of the existing vacant positions, and no new units should be established unless deemed necessary.

In filling positions of civil servants and workers in public organisations vacant as of 31 December 1993 and any such positions that have become vacant since that date, for any reason, priority should be given to transferring personnel from the units with surplus personnel and from organisations covered by the privatisation programme.

The civil servants' salary adjustment system was changed. Instead of semi-annual increases, salaries will be raised on a quarterly basis, effective from July 1993.

The compulsory saving scheme rates were reduced from 6 per cent and 4 per cent to 3 per cent and 2 per cent respectively, effective from 15 January 1994.

The spending agencies (except for State economic enterprises and local authorities) are required to get approval (visa) from the Ministry of Finance for the positions of both civil servants and workers.

The wage budget was introduced this year in order to discipline the wage and overtime payments for workers (caps on wages of temporary workers and on the overtime payments of both permanent and temporary workers).

Starting in 1994, the positions of civil servants and workers of municipalities are now subjected to visa (approval) of the Ministry of the Interior.

A part-time employment system for university students in the administration of universities was introduced in 1993.

All government procurement over a certain limit set in budget law are subjected to visa of the Ministry of Finance (excluding local authorities and extra-budgetary funds).

Fifty-nine of the extra-budgetary funds were integrated into the budget to control their incomes and expenditures and to ensure fiscal discipline.

A limit was brought by the Ministry of the Interior to all expenditures of municipalities with a total of salaries exceeding 30 per cent of their income.

The honorariums of the members of the municipal assemblies of cities with a population of over 70 000 are subject to the visa of the Ministry of the Interior.

Privatisation

The Turkish Privatisation Programme, started in 1984, is presently executed by the Public Participation Administration (PPA). Currently the PPA is vested with the authority to conduct the privatisation of the State-owned companies, subsidiaries and minority shares, manage the Public Participation Fund, and finance major infrastructure projects.

From 1986 through the end of 1993, a total of 126 State-owned companies, subsidiaries and equity participations have been privatised either by block sale, domestic or international public offering, or stock sales via the Istanbul Stock Exchange. The total sales proceeds during this period were about US$1.7 billion.

Work on privatisation continues. The speed of privatisation activities in Turkey will increase in exponential terms according to projected revenues. In accordance with the budgets prepared by the PPA for the years 1994 and 1995, approximately US$2.6 and US$18 billion are planned to be generated as privatisation income respectively. Over the next four years, the PPA aims to privatise at least 30 per cent of the State shares.

Parallel to this, in order to accelerate privatisation applications and improve their efficiency, establish their integrity and avoid their complexity, and to enable prompt decision-making, some structural changes in the legal and social areas will be made next year.

Commercialisation or corporatisation of public bodies

The fees for social facilities and the rents for government housing were increased by about 150 per cent in early 1994. The student contribution fees for universities were increased by more than 100 per cent.

Decentralisation to sub-national government

Town and city assemblies which were established in 1992 are still active, also fulfilling an important role in improving relations with citizens.

Use of market-type mechanisms

Government agencies are encouraged to contract out cleaning and catering services to the private sector (particularly in hospitals and universities).

Other main fields of public management reform

Personnel management

Public personnel whose average assessment grade for the last six years is 90 or above (out of 100) can get an extra step increase; and those who have reached the highest step in their grade can get promoted to the next grade.

Successful civil servants and contracted personnel can get one or two additional salaries in a year, as a performance bonus, on the proposal of their senior managers.

As from 1987, public personnel have been receiving foreign language compensation for each language they speak. This initiative aims to encourage public personnel to learn foreign languages. Currently, personnel can take level tests in 19 different foreign languages. As a result of the level tests, held twice a year in May and November, entrants are categorised into three different grades, A, B and C. The rate of compensation varies according to the grade received.

Professional development courses for civil servants in the public sector still continue, both in the country and abroad.

Regulatory management and reform, and management of information technology

Codification of 11 259 laws and regulations since the foundation of the Republic, a process which was started in 1985 and completed in 1988, is continuously updated by the use of a ''loose-leaf'' system to include laws and regulations which come into force.

All valid laws and regulations are registered in a computer database and made available through a network.

The most recently enacted laws, regulations, bids and adjudications published in the Official Gazette are broadcast daily on a teletext programme by the Turkish Radio and Television Corporation to serve the aim of informing the public of government decisions.

Most of the public institutions now use information technology.

Considering the importance of the training programmes on information technology, the State Personnel Presidency organised several seminars for high and mid-level managers from various public organisations.

In 1993, 174 managers in total attended the following seminars:

– the use of computers in management;
– basic principles of effective management and administration;
– human relations in management and managerial behaviour;
– decision-making in management;
– creative management to deal with changes;
– new approaches in human resource management;
– ergonomics;
– quality-cost-productivity;
– obtaining effective teamwork;
– ways to successful management;
– change management.

Improving relations with citizens/enterprises

The requests for information from citizens and their opinions on various subjects are taken into consideration and transferred to related authorities daily in the central government.

UNITED KINGDOM

Limits to the size of the public sector

Reducing the public sector

As part of its policy of reducing public sector activities to essential tasks and ensuring that these are efficiently managed, the Government has strengthened procedures for conducting quinquennial reviews of the functions of executive non-departmental public bodies (NDPBs). All decisions on the future of large executive NDPBs (on whether their function should be abolished, privatised, contracted-out, or retained within the public sector) will be referred to ministers in central departments for agreement. Decisions on small NDPBs may be referred to ministers. This will bring procedures for executive NDPBs more closely in line with the triennial reviews of Next Steps executive agencies.

For both Next Steps agencies and large executive NDPBs, advance announcement of a review, inviting outside contribution, is required. Departments are encouraged to take a similar approach for new agency candidates.

Spending

The Government has announced a freeze on departments' running costs in 1994/95, as part of its continuing efforts to improve efficiency and cut waste. Departments will also be expected to keep their pay budgets (60 per cent of total running costs) to their 1993/94 level (except where significant workload changes are demonstrated), and to finance any increase in pay in 1994/95 through improvements in productivity. For 1995/96 and 1996/97, cash provision for running costs will be broadly held to the same level. As a result, running costs are expected to reduce from 8.2 per cent of public expenditure in 1993/94, to 7.4 per cent in 1996/97.

Commercialisation of public bodies/deconcentration within central government

By end of 1993, 92 executive agencies had been launched (employing 60 per cent of all civil servants). The target is to complete the programme by mid 1995 with about 75 per cent of Home Civil Service employees working in organisations operating under Next Steps principles (in Northern Ireland, where the programme started later, completion will be by mid-1996).

The Next Steps Review: 1993, published in December 1993, includes:

- agencies overall met 77 per cent of key targets (which are made more robust each year) set for 1992/93, an improvement on previous years;
- 16 agencies were launched (including HM Prison Service and the Social Security Child Support Agency);
- tables documenting the progress towards completion of periodic agency reviews.

All agencies are now required to prepare commercial-style accruals accounts within two years of launch.

Use of market-type mechanisms

From 1 April 1992 to 31 December 1993, about £1.1 billion of central government activity has been market-tested or otherwise examined to see how value for money can best be improved. Full details, including estimated savings from the programme, were set out in the *Citizen's Charter Second Report* published in March 1994.

Personnel management

The application of uniform terms and conditions to the diverse group of civil service organisations is no longer appropriate. The Civil Service (Management Functions) Act 1992 empowers the Treasury and Cabinet Office (OPSS) to delegate selectively to departments and agencies responsibility for determining specific terms and conditions of their staff, or delegate functions generally to departments and agencies. Departments and agencies have now become empowered to determine a wider range of terms and conditions of their own staff, subject to any conditions applied in the delegation, without further reference to the central departments. From 1 April 1994, twenty-one agencies, plus HM Customs and Excise and the Inland Revenue, will take on responsibility for their pay and related conditions of service. Agencies with over 500 staff have been invited to put forward their own proposals on pay and pay related conditions of service which are more appropriate to their business needs by 1 April 1995.

An increasing number of government departments and agencies are joining a scheme which uses external assessment against a national standard to assess the effectiveness of their investment in training and development. The scheme (Investors in People) is being promoted by Government to both public and private sector organisations as a means to improve their overall performance.

Improving relations with citizens/enterprises

The Citizen's Charter ten-year programme continued to gather momentum during 1993, with the aim of raising the standard of public services and making them more responsive to users. The number of charters covering individual services rose to 38. Most of the main areas of public service are now covered by published statements of service standards. Some of the first charters are being revised with higher standards, *e.g.* the London Underground Rail Charter and HM Customs and Excise Charter for Travellers.

A Citizen's Charter survey, published in September 1993, showed that 70 per cent of people were aware of the Citizen's Charter and believed it would help raise standards of public service.

The Charter initiative was promoted during the year by:

- the award of 93 Charter Marks for excellence in delivering public services in line with Citizen's Charter principles. Over 400 applications for the award showed an increase of more than 100 on the first year of the scheme when 36 awards were made;
- the launch of the Citizen's Charter Complaint Task Force, to undertake a wide-ranging two-year review of public service complaints systems to ensure that they operate in line with Charter principles;
- a series of Charter Forums held around the country for service deliverers to promote implementation of the Charter and exchange of best practice;
- the launch of a free quarterly magazine, "Charter News", distributed to over 100 000 public sector managers;
- a second successful international conference, "Service for the Citizen", in December 1993, attended by more than 200 delegates from 20 countries who discussed ways of raising the standard of public sector performance.

Deregulation

The Deregulation Initiative, launched in 1985 with the aim of significantly reducing administrative and regulatory burdens on business, has three main objectives:

- **better existing regulation**, by cutting unnecessary burdens on business and reducing compliance and enforcement costs;

- **effective new regulation**, by taking account of the views of business, and of the potential burdens on business, when framing, implementing and enforcing new regulation and in negotiating EU proposals; and
- **greater official awareness of the views and need of business**, through better consultation and communication.

In a renewed drive in 1992, the President of the Board of Trade was given specific responsibility to tackle the problems that the accumulation of regulation imposed on the wealth creation process. A comprehensive list of some 3 500 regulations which imposed costs on business was identified. Government departments were asked to identify candidates for repeal or simplification.

In February 1993, the Government decided to set up seven task forces of business people to conduct an independent review of regulation. Their remit also included advising on the most effective way of developing, introducing and enforcing new regulations. The task forces produced their findings in September 1993 and the proposals for reform, 605 in total, were published by the Government in January 1994. Two documents outlining the principles for good regulation were published (*A Guide to Good Regulation* and *Guidance on the Use of Risk Assessment*), and a successor Deregulation Task Force was authorised to investigate complaints of excessive regulation or enforcement directly with government departments and to ensure that the principles of good regulations are being applied to new regulations.

The Government has announced that during 1994 Parliament will consider legislative proposals to facilitate the implementation of the deregulation programme.

Access to official information

The Government has re-affirmed its commitment to openness by instituting a voluntary Code of Practice on access to government information. This commits government departments and other public bodies to release background information with major policy announcements, to give reasons for their decisions and to provide other information on request. The independent Parliamentary Commissioner for Administration will be able to investigate complaints about non-disclosure, and make recommendations. The Government also proposes to introduce legislation providing the right of access to government information relating to human health and safety and, for the individual, to personal records held by government.

UNITED STATES

Size and structure of the public sector

Limits to the size of the public sector

The Administration is requiring agencies to eliminate 252 000 federal positions over the next five years, representing a 12 per cent reduction in federal employment. Passage of the Budget Enforcement Act of 1993 established spending caps through fiscal year 1997 that place a ceiling on federal spending.

Decentralisation to sub-national government

The President's Community Enterprise Board, composed of selected Cabinet members, agency heads and major policy advisors, was established to help start a bottom-up grant consolidation effort for 104 communities across the country. The Board will develop recommendations for administrative and legislative actions aimed at providing communities with the flexibility to spend federal funds on locally-determined needs.

Use of market-type mechanisms

The federal government continues to rely on user fees to cover the cost of operations in selected areas. A major new fee will be introduced this year by the Federal Communications Commission for licensing of electromagnetic frequencies previously unavailable to the private sector.

Other restructuring or "rationalisation" efforts

The Vice-President led the National Performance Review (NPR), a comprehensive review of the federal government to determine both government-wide and programme-specific actions that can be taken to restructure and streamline government operations. The NPR developed 384 recommendations, encompassing 1 211 individual actions. (Many of the initiatives summarised in this chapter were either conceived or endorsed by the NPR.)

The major areas in which the NPR made recommendations include quality leadership and management, management control, organisational structure and programme design, customer service, performance budgeting, financial management, human resource management, procurement, support services, information technology, intergovernmental partnership, environmental management, and regulatory systems.

Other main fields of public management reform

Management of policy-making

The administration established the National Economic Council, composed of Cabinet members, certain agency heads and top policy advisors to the President, to co-ordinate the development, analysis and implementation of the Government's economic policy-making with regard to domestic and international issues. The National Science and Technology Council, composed of federal agencies, was established to co-ordinate the Government's science and technology policy and budget-making process.

Performance management

The Government Performance and Results Act (GPRA) was enacted, requiring agencies to develop strategic plans (by 1997), prepare annual performance goal plans (by 1997), and report actual performance against goals (by 2000). The act will also provide agencies with waivers for certain administrative requirements to allow greater management flexibility in exchange for greater accountability. A number of agencies are being selected as GPRA pilot projects for 1994, 1995 and 1996. Agencies selected for pilot projects will prepare performance plans and programme performance reports and receive administrative waivers.

Financial resources management

The Federal Accounting Standards Advisory Board developed recommendations that would establish standards for government accounting of direct loans and loan guarantees, inventories and other related properties, and assets and liabilities. The Board also developed a statement on the objectives of federal financial reporting.

Personnel management

A National Partnership Council was established to promote a greater sense of co-operation between management and federal employee labour unions, and to draft legislation that will enable a stronger labour-management partnership. Additionally, the NPR recommended that the Federal Personnel Manual be abolished.

Regulatory management and reform

The administration directed all agencies to conduct a review of regulations, eliminate one-half of executive branch internal regulations, and take steps to put the regulatory review process more in the public light. The administration has also directed all agencies to conduct at least one rule-making through the negotiated rule-making (reg-neg) process, and to streamline their regulatory development process.

Improving relations with citizens/enterprises

Federal agencies that deliver services are now required to identify and survey customers and set customer service standards. The authority to approve surveys, which had been held by the Office of Management and Budget, was delegated to the agency heads to reduce the administrative barriers in determining customer needs. Several agencies, such as the Internal Revenue Service, the Social Security Administration, and the Postal Service, have developed customer service standards.

Other

The administration is promoting the exchange of procurement information, such as invoices, electronically between the federal government and the private sector.

Annex 1
STATISTICS

This year, the enquiry for the Update included a special effort to improve the statistical content of the annual survey. For this reason, the statistical tables are collected in this annex to facilitate an overview of results. An improved comparability across countries was aimed for, by trying to obtain data according to the concept of "general government" of the System of National Accounts (SNA). It became evident that not all countries adhere to this concept and that, when they do, the set of employment data in their national accounts provides very few breakdowns.

For these reasons, initiatives were taken to explore other statistical sources to gather more disaggregated public employment data which are at the same time comparable across countries. Most of these sources are based in national statistical offices. Standardised industrial or institutional classifications compatible with, or convertible to, ISIC (International Standard Industrial Classification) are available in which the notions of the government and public sectors are based on internationally agreed criteria. Therefore, for some countries, new tables have been added along with the explanations necessary to understand the differences in concepts used.

The continuing work in this area has the goal of compiling a set of data of good comparability on public sector employment at different levels of disaggregation for all OECD countries, beginning from 1980. At the present stage, cross-country comparisons of the data provided in this annex must still be interpreted with great care.

AUSTRALIA

Introduction

The following tables provide data from two different sources. Table 1 stems from the Department of Finance which registers staff employed either permanently or temporarily under the Public Service Act 1922 at federal department or agency level. Table 2 provides data from the Australian Bureau of Statistics (ABS) based on the Standard Institutional Sector Classification of Australia (SISCA). This classification uses the public sector concept which is composed of general government enterprises, public trading enterprises and public financial institutions. General government enterprises correspond to the general government concept of the SNA (System of National Accounts). However, permanent defence forces are excluded. Table 3 provides data, also from the Australian Board of Statistics, based on the Australian Standard Industrial Classification (ASIC) which uses the notion of public administration and defence. However, data for all ''industries'' are also cross-tabulated by institutional sector.

Table 1.1.   **Federal administration employment (detailed)**

(permanent and temporary staff in June)

	1992			1993 [1]		
	Depts. (%)	Agencies (%)	TOTAL (No.)	Depts. (%)	Agencies (%)	TOTAL (No.)
Prime Minister and Cabinet	51	49	992	17	83	2 794
House of Representatives	–	–	–	100	0	234
Senate	–	–	–	100	0	246
Joint House	–	–	–	100	0	366
Parliamentary library and reporting staff	–	–	–	100	0	469
Administrative Services [2]	94	6	11 940	88	12	10 853
Attorney General	47	53	6 462	48	52	7 232
Defence [3]	99	1	22 597	99	1	20 452
Employment, Education and Training	89	11	14 044	100	0	15 306
Finance	43	57	2 095	48	52	1 995
Foreign Affairs and Trade	87	13	4 569	87	13	4 494
Health, Housing and Community Services [4]	31	69	19 313	35	65	18 909
Immigration and Ethnic Affairs [5]	100	0	2 871	100	0	3 514
Industrial Relations	46	54	1 719	45	55	1 862
Industry, Technology and Regional Development	25	75	6 632	25	75	6 484
Primary Industries and Energy	100	0	4 182	100	0	3 926
Social Security	100	0	19 942	100	0	22 112
Sport, Environment and Territories [6]	30	70	4 037	27	73	2 900
Tourism	100	0	155	100	0	138
Transport and Communications	56	44	3 300	51	49	3 142
Treasury	2	98	24 185	2	98	23 013
TOTAL			149 035			150 441

– Not available.
1.   1993 figures do not include Australian Capital Territory Public Service.
2.   Includes Arts in 1993.
3.   Civilian staff only.
4.   Includes local government in 1993.
5.   Includes local government in 1992.
6.   Includes Arts in 1992.
Source: Australian Public Service Statistical Bulletin, Department of Finance.

Table 1.2. **Federal administration (totals)** [1]

(permanent and temporary staff in June)

	1980	(%)	1985	(%)	1992	(%)	1993 [2]	(%)
Departments	123 456	(80)	138 737	(80)	93 682	(63)	96 912	(64)
Agencies attached	29 973	(20)	34 927	(20)	55 353	(37)	53 529	(36)
TOTAL	153 429	(100)	173 664	(100)	149 035	(100)	150 441	(100)

1. The portfolio, departmental and agency list was substantially changed in 1987 and 1993. As such, it is not possible to provide detailed breakdowns as in Table 1.1 for 1980 and 1985.
2. 1993 figures do not include the Australian Capital Territory Public Service.
Sources: Public Service Board Statistical Yearbook 1980 and 1984/85; Australian Public Service Statistical Bulletin 1992/93.

Table 2. **Employed wage and salary earners by public institutional sector** [1]

(head count, full-time plus part-time)

	February 1985	February 1992	February 1993	of which:		
				General government enterprises [2]	*Public trading enterprises*	*Public financial institutions*
Commonwealth	429 000	401 700	383 600	*182 500*	*149 600*	*51 500*
State	1 077 000	1 113 400	1 084 800	*905 600*	*152 900*	*26 300*
Local	152 000	161 900	162 000	*147 200*	*14 800*	*0*
TOTAL PUBLIC SECTOR	1 658 000	1 677 000	1 630 400	*1 235 300*	*317 300*	*77 800*

1. Excludes permanent defence forces.
2. Includes all "Public Service Act" staff.
Sources: Employed Wage and Salary Earners, March Quarter, 1985, 1992, 1993, Australian Bureau of Statistics.

Table 3. **Employed wage and salary earners by industry classified in the public sector**

(head count, full-time plus part-time)

	March 1985	March 1992	March 1993
Public administration and defence [1]	*	*	*
Community services:	721 000	829 400	827 400
Health	*266 500*	*289 900*	*288 100*
Education, museum and library services	*351 800*	*399 600*	*397 400*
Welfare and religious institutions	*–*	*24 100*	*24 900*
Other	*102 700*	*115 800*	*117 000*
Other industries in the public sector [2]	*	*	*
TOTAL PUBLIC SECTOR	*	*	*

* Data not supplied.
– Data not available.
1. Excluding permanent defence forces.
2. For example, transport and storage, communications; finance, property and business services.
Sources: Employed Wage and Salary Earners, March Quarter, 1985, 1992, 1993, Australian Bureau of Statistics.

AUSTRIA

Table 1. **Federal public employees by ministry**

	1992	1993
Federal Chancellery	2 360	2 315
Agriculture and Forestry	5 905	3 797
Defence [1]	23 179	21 949
Economic Affairs	7 204	6 408
Education and Art	40 842	42 575
Environment, Youth and Family	579	561
Finances	25 055	19 861
Foreign Affairs	1 577	1 525
Health Affairs, Consumer Protection and Sports [2]	1 549	1 495
Interior	31 504	31 613
Justice	11 263	11 461
Public Economy and Transport	1 503	1 470
Science and Research	21 064	21 381
Social Affairs and Labour	5 315	5 648
TOTAL	178 899	172 059

1.   Defence administration plus soldiers.
2.   In 1992 and 1993, Health Affairs and Sports.
Sources: Budget figures from the Ministry of Finance for 1992; effective numbers from the Personalinformationssystem des Bundes, the Post and Telegraph administration and the Austrian Federal Railways for 1993.

Table 2. **Federal public employees in other bodies**

	1992	1993
Chancellery of the Federal President	66	72
Parliament	310	319
Federal theatres	2 801	2 837
Austrian Federal Forests	2 961	961
Post and Telegraph Administration	59 288	58 440
Austrian Federal Railways	66 873	66 350
Other	591	592
TOTAL	132 890	129 571

Sources: Budget figures from the Ministry of Finance for 1992; effective numbers from the Personalinformationssystem des Bundes for 1993, the Post and Telegraph Administration and the Austrian Railways.

Table 3. **Public employees by level of government**

	1990	1991	1992/93
Federal	308 789	308 270	301 630[1]
Länder	159 200	145 649	146 183[2]
Municipalities	71 269	74 218	76 252[2]
Vienna	67 490	62 539	66 797[2]
TOTAL	606 748	590 676	590 862

1. Figure for 1993.
2. Figures for 1992.

Sources: Personalinformationssystem des Bundes for federal employment; Central Statistical Office for *Länder,* municipalities and Vienna.

BELGIUM

Introduction

The tables below are based on three very different data sources. The first three are provided by the Ministry of the Interior and of Public Administration. The composition of the public sector is given in Tables 2 and 3. It includes notably the personnel of autonomous public enterprises, teaching staff (including from subsidised educational institutes) and professional military (excluding conscripts). Table 4 presents data based on the standardised ESA classification: European System of Integrated Economic Accounts which is convertible to the System of National Accounts (SNA) of the United Nations and which uses the concept of General Government. Table 5 is based on the standard european industrial classification NACE and cross-tabulates by institutional sector.

Table 1. **Public employees by ministry**

	June 1980	June 1985	December 1991	December 1992
Prime Minister	859	508	576	598
Agriculture	2 529	1 785	1 077	1 062
Brussels Region	–	168	–	–
Communications and Public Works[1]	12 085	10 860	1 507	1 520
Economic Affairs	3 505	3 230	3 552	3 427
Employment and Labour	1 602	1 683	1 535	1 491
Finance	36 205	37 040	32 505	32 557
Foreign Affairs, Foreign Trade and Development Co-operation[2]	3 782	3 668	1 716	1 678
Interior and Public Service[3]	2 468	2 602	2 362	2 277
Justice	6 830	6 626	6 365	6 420
Middle Classes (self employed)	488	327	313	317
National Defence	9 709	7 208	4 084	3 997
National Education[4]	3 963	3 647	84	85
Public Health and Environment[5]	3 305	1 674	1 345	1 328
Social Affairs	732	746	807	823
TOTAL[6]	88 062	81 772	57 828	57 580

– Not available.
1. In 1980, Communications and Post and Telephone; and Public Works. In 1985, Communications and Public Works. In 1991, Communications and Post and Telephone; and Public Works. For technical reasons, contract staff under "Public Works" is not included in the figures.
2. In 1980, Foreign Affairs.
3. In 1980, Interior.
4. In 1980, National Education and French Culture plus *Nationale Opvoeding en Nederlandse Cultuur.*
5. In 1985, Public Health and the Family.
6. For 1985 and 1991, any comparison with 1980 figures should take into account the transfer of staff to the Communities and the Regions.
Source: "Aperçu des effectifs du secteur public", ministère de l'Intérieur et de la Fonction publique.

Table 2. **Personnel in other State institutions**

	June 1980	June 1985	December 1991	December 1992
State scientific establishments	–	–	3 092	3 087
National public interest bodies[1]	198 402	184 841	159 458	155 048
Special bodies:	87 434	86 172	78 855	77 747
Judiciary	*8 027*	*8 268*	*9 666*	*9 934*
Council of State	*195*	*236*	*265*	*314*
Provincial governors and regional tax collectors	*300*	*274*	*296*	*284*
Army[2]	*63 407*	*61 273*	*51 526*	*50 162*
Gendarmerie	*15 505*	*16 121*	*17 102*	*17 053*
Teaching personnel[3]	304 902	268 114	0	0
Legislative authorities	1 232	1 392	1 880	1 959
TOTAL[4]	591 970	540 519	243 285	237 841

– Not available.
1. Includes autonomous public enterprises (Belgacom, La Poste, SNCB, CGER and Crédit communal).
2. Only career military personnel.
3. Transferred to the Communities in 1991 and 1992.
4. For 1985 and 1991, any comparison with 1980 figures should take into account the transfer of staff to the Communities and the Regions.
Source: "Aperçu des effectifs du secteur public", ministère de l'Intérieur et de la Fonction publique.

Table 3. **Personnel by level of Government**

	June 1980	June 1985	December 1991	December 1992
Central	680 032	622 291	301 113	295 421
Communities and Regions:	–	12 567	344 140	352 438
Ministries	–	–	*23 301*	*24 228*
Scientific establishments	–	–	*193*	*204*
Public interest bodies	–	–	*43 214*	*46 781*
Teaching personnel	–	–	*277 432*	*281 225*
Provincial and local administrations[1]	184 643	181 058	239 924	237 368
TOTAL GOVERNMENT SECTOR	864 675	815 916	885 177	885 227

– Not available.
1. In 1980 and 1985, local authorities (including municipalities, public social aid centres, and provinces).
Source: "Aperçu des effectifs du secteur public", ministère de l'Intérieur et de la Fonction publique.

Table 4. **Total employment in General Government**

	1980	1985	1991	1992
Public administrations	700 500	727 400	730 700	724 900

Source: National Statistical Office (INS) using labour force data provided by the Ministry of Employment and Work. This source uses the ESA classification (European System of integrated Accounts). The branch "General Government" does not include personnel in public enterprises, but it includes military (professionals and conscripts).

Table 5. **Internal employment by activity branch and by sector**

	1980	1985	1991
TOTAL PUBLIC SECTOR	948 487	964 890	967 431
Including:			
General administration and compulsory social			
security[1]	*211 828*	*216 510*	*208 630*
Armed forces[2]	*90 345*	*89 300*	*83 875*
Education	*264 046*	*268 639*	*270 951*

1. Including Parliament, justice and public order.
2. Including conscripts.
Source: Ministry of Employment and Work in ''La population active en Belgique'', Vol. 2, historical data post 1970. This source uses the NACE (Nomenclature des activités dans la Communauté européenne) classification .

CANADA

Introduction

The following tables provide data from two different sources. Table 1 is published by the Public Service Commission and records only federal government employees subject to the Public Service Employment Act. Table 2 adds other employees at the federal level including personnel in federal government enterprises. Table 3 is published by Statistics Canada, Public Institutions Division. The notion of government in this source is identical to the concept of general government of the SNA (System of National Accounts). It excludes public enterprises.

Table 1. **Public service employees**

	1980	1985	1991	1992
Agriculture	9 215	11 177	9 898	10 453
Atlantic Canada Opportunities Agency	–	–	337	372
Bureau of Pensions Advocates	209	124	126	94
Canadian Grain Commission	807	736	747	779
Canadian Human Rights Commission	104	152	218	225
Canadian International Development Agency	973	1 169	1 193	1 281
Canadian Radio-Television and Telecommunications Commission	378	396	407	414
Canadian Space Agency	–	–	213	268
Canadian Transportation Investigation and Safety Board	–	–	278	292
Communications	1 952	2 237	2 247	2 397
Consumer and Corporate Affairs	2 127	2 393	2 209	2 291
Correctional Service Canada	9 981	10 721	10 140	10 566
Employment and Immigration	22 894	24 466	24 438	25 596
Energy, Mines and Resources	3 491	4 972	3 959	3 965
Environment	–	9 163	9 128	9 533
External Affairs	2 933	4 380	4 158	4 263
Federal Court	128	176	273	342
Finance	623	878	911	916
Fisheries and Oceans	4 992	5 881	5 626	5 547
Forestry	–	–	1 270	1 361
Immigration and Refugee Board[1]	47	68	709	730
Indian Affairs and Northern Development	6 009	5 478	3 692	3 705
Industry, Science and Technology[2]	2 422	98	2 146	1 992
Investment Canada	–	123	112	111
Justice	1 122	1 373	1 943	2 149
Labour	780	787	902	912
Multiculturalism and Citizenship	–	–	272	669
National Archives of Canada	701	810	772	784
National Defence (civilian)	33 924	33 827	30 760	31 092
National Energy Board	–	411	232	304
National Health and Welfare	8 337	9 473	8 336	8 766
National Library of Canada	463	536	516	528
National Parole Board	225	265	272	289
National Revenue (Customs and Excise)[3]	23 630	9 802	13 265	13 832
National Revenue (Taxation)[3]	–	17 122	20 839	21 729
National Transportation Agency of Canada[4]	780	776	475	495
Office of Federal-Provincial Relations	68	54	101	138
Office of the Commissioner of Official Languages	100	140	165	173
Office of the Secretary to the Governor General	84	102	113	125
Office of the Superintendent of Financial Institutions	–	–	385	386
Privy Council Office	258	367	408	446
Public Service Commission	2 512	2 563	1 968	2 017
Public Service Staff Relations Board	156	155	141	82
Public Works	8 227	7 851	7 140	7 214
Royal Canadian Mounted Police (public service employees)	3 512	3 348	3 389	3 386
Secretary of State of Canada	–	3 050	2 537	2 206
Solicitor General	–	305	295	312
Statistics Canada	4 343	4 603	4 707	4 814
Supply and Services	9 433	10 139	8 614	8 757
Supreme Court	55	67	135	137
Tax Court of Canada	–	57	110	126
Transport	19 271	21 027	19 081	18 601
Treasury Board (Office of the Comptroller General)	–	151	140	141
Treasury Board Secretariat	–	785	655	648
Veterans Affairs	3 744	3 312	3 586	3 542
Western Economic Diversification	–	–	274	280
Other[5]	77 129	5 127	855	1 025
TOTAL	268 139	223 173	217 818	223 598

– Data not available.
1.   Immigration Appeal Board in 1980 and 1985.
2.   Industry, Trade and Commerce in 1980; Science and Technology in 1985.
3.   Customs, Excise and Taxation in 1980.
4.   Canadian Transport Commission in 1980 and 1985.
5.   Including all bodies which had less than 100 staff in 1991.
Source: Public Service Commission.

Table 2.   **Federal government employment**

	December 1985	December 1991	December 1992
Public servants (Public Service Commission)	223 173	217 818	223 598
Personnel employed by the Treasury Board	14 285	17 109	–
National Defence military personnel	87 017	86 319	–
Personnel of other corporations and agencies not employed by the Treasury Board	32 760	33 109	–
Royal Canadian Mounted Police (uniformed personnel)	18 428	19 521	–
Personnel of government enterprises	212 622	155 828	–
TOTAL	588 285	529 704	–

– Data not available.
Source: Public Service Commission.

Table 3.   **Government employment by level**

	1987	1990	1991	1992
Federal government administration [1]	397 534	408 885	418 482	412 797
of which: Military [2]	*113 394*	*118 779*	*121 410*	*117 461*
Provincial/territorial government:	901 632	952 527	965 646	964 138
Provincial/territorial administration [3]	*515 165*	*534 409*	*535 116*	*539 411*
Public hospitals [4]	*386 467*	*418 118*	*430 531*	*424 728*
Local government:	841 023	924 896	944 969	964 040
Local government administration	*326 649*	*358 853*	*366 094*	*373 019*
Local hospitals [5]	*63 271*	*67 685*	*67 655*	*67 033*
Local school boards	*451 103*	*498 358*	*511 220*	*523 988*
TOTAL GOVERNMENT	2 140 188	2 286 307	2 329 097	2 340 976
Total government administration	*1 239 348*	*1 302 146*	*1 319 692*	*1 325 226*
Total hospitals	*449 737*	*485 804*	*498 185*	*491 761*
Total local school boards	*451 103*	*498 358*	*511 220*	*523 988*

1.   Includes military, government-owned hospitals and education (except universities).
2.   Includes regular and reserve forces.
3.   Includes government-owned hospitals and community colleges.
4.   Hospitals under control of a government.
5.   Municipally-owned hospitals.
Source: Public Institutions Division, Statistics Canada.

DENMARK

Introduction

The statistics in Tables 1 to 3 were provided by the Ministry of Finance. According to this source, the **government** sector is composed of the State administration, the county administration, the municipalities, and the Church plus institutions owned by these authorities such as schools, hospitals, museums, research centres and some State-owned enterprises (*e.g.* Danish Railways and Danish Postal Services). Included in the government sector are: teachers in public institutions, the army (professional soldiers but not conscripts) and the police. The **public** sector includes in addition part of the subsidised sector (*Tilskudomradet*), *i.e.* private and independent institutions where more than half of the receipts come from public subsidies.

Tables 1 to 3 are for the public sector. They do not permit the separation of employment for the government sector.

Table 4 is new. It is based on data from Statistics Denmark using an industrial classification. The concept of producers of government services (industrial class 98099) is very close to the SNA general government concept, and indeed the figures in this table correspond to the ones that the OECD has on Denmark.

Table 1.   **Public employment at the State level by ministry**

(full-time equivalents)

	1990	1991	1992		
			Ministries	Directorates, institutions and State enterprises	TOTAL[6]
Prime Minister's Office	111	113	66	51	117
Agriculture	3 310	3 303	140	3 245	3 385
Communications[1]	33 053	27 731	249	25 819	26 068
Cultural Affairs	3 682	3 626	142	3 469	3 611
Defence[2]	33 528	31 835	143	30 822	30 966
Ecclesiastical Affairs	65	52	40	11	51
Economic Affairs	871	613	33	567	599
Education and Research[3]	33 188	35 212	698	36 034	36 733
Energy	1 319	1 249	70	1 172	1 242
Environment	2 562	2 619	88	2 545	2 633
Finance	939	852	310	495	805
Fiscal Affairs	6 756	6 409	169	6 074	6 243
Fisheries	598	590	150	400	551
Foreign Affairs	1 409	1 435	1 474	9	1 482
Health	9 774	9 256	103	7 977	8 080
Housing	2 150	2 098	81	1 929	2 010
Industry	1 831	1 761	121	1 507	1 628
Interior and Nordic Affairs	1 463	1 428	111	1 605	1 717
Justice[4]	21 001	20 741	216	20 450	20 666
Labour	6 017	5 655	148	5 696	5 844
Social Affairs	1 836	1 678	291	1 396	1 687
Transport[5]	25 078	24 139	88	23 915	24 003
TOTAL[6]	190 541	182 395	4 932	175 187	180 119

1.   Includes staff of Danish Postal Services.
2.   Includes professional military but not conscripts.
3.   Includes teachers.
4.   Includes police.
5.   Includes staff of Danish Railways.
6.   Totals may not add up due to rounding.
Source: Ministry of Finance.

Table 2.   **Public sector employment by level of government**

(full-time equivalents)

	1990	1991	1992
State	191 000	182 396	180 119
County	127 300	128 244	127 658
Municipalities	302 900	312 334	317 465
Copenhagen and Frederiksberg	69 400	69 999	65 653
TOTAL	690 600	692 973	690 895

Source: Ministry of Finance.

Table 3.   **Public sector employment by function of government**

(percentages)

	1980	1990	1991	1992
Management of the public sector	5.5	5.3	10.0	9.9
Social welfare	27.0	29.3	26.9	27.2
Health	16.0	14.9	16.2	16.0
Education and research	21.0	20.6	18.5	18.6
Culture and church	2.5	2.3	2.1	2.1
Transport and communication	12.0	10.4	9.8	9.1
Environment and housing	2.2	2.2	2.2	2.4
Electricity, gas, water and heating	1.0	1.0	0.8	0.8
Justice	3.2	3.3	3.0	3.0
Defence	5.7	4.9	4.6	4.5
Other purposes	4.3	5.8	5.9	6.4
TOTAL	100.0	100.0	100.0	100.0

Source: Ministry of Finance.

Table 4.   **Employment in ''producers of government services''**

(number of persons)

	1980	1985	1989
Producers of government services	610 958	751 715	780 012

Source: Statistics Denmark.

FINLAND

Introduction

The tables below are based on two different sources. Tables 1 to 5 are based on figures provided by the State's Employer Office of the Ministry of Finance. Table 6 is new. It is based on the figures provided by Statistics Finland in the Labour Force Survey. This source uses a standard industrial classification (SIC) and cross tabulates data by employer sector. The SIC (version of 1988) contains (class 81 and 83), Public Administration and Defence and the public employer sector is broken down into state and local. Both sources exclude conscripts from the labour force.

Table 1. **Public employees in Ministries** [1]

	1980	1985	1991	1992
Office of the President	41	50	62	61
Parliament (officials)	–	–	379	386
Office of the Council of State	168	166	124	128
Agriculture and Forestry	110	124	269	263
Transport and Communications	101	110	146	146
Defence	260	288	235	236
Education	207	287	292	268
Environment [2]	–	233	259	263
Finance	337	356	299	298
Foreign Affairs [3]	1 182	1 590	1 793	1 676
Interior	318	228	316	305
Justice	349	383	442	438
Labour	263	278	304	301
Social Affairs and Health	217	257	255	318
Trade and Industry	243	256	287	302
TOTAL	3 796	4 606	5 462	5 389

– Data not available.
1. Employees in agencies not included in this table.
2. This ministry was established in 1983.
3. Including embassies in foreign countries.
Source: Tietoja valtion henkilöstöstä 1970-1992 (Facts about central government personnel, No. 20), the State Employer's Office, Ministry of Finance.

Table 2.   **State sector[1] personnel by Ministerial branch**

	1980	1985	1991	1992
Office of the President	41	50	62	61
Parliament	–	–	379	386
Office of the Council of State	200	203	209	213
Agriculture and Forestry	6 760	7 889	8 365	10 780
of which: State enterprises	–	–	*140*	*145*
Transport and Communications	94 540	89 464	77 966	73 076
of which: State enterprises	–	–	*61 401*	*56 977*
Defence[2]	20 390	24 526	21 338	21 304
Education[3]	21 315	28 417	35 873	35 751
Environment	2 424	2 843	3 036	2 924
Finance	16 744	19 109	19 571	19 165
of which: State enterprises	–	–	*3 417*	*3 177*
Foreign Affairs	1 182	1 590	1 847	1 676
Interior[4]	17 750	18 757	19 059	19 165
Justice[5]	6 190	6 809	7 659	7 681
Labour	2 929	3 263	4 381	4 540
Social Affairs and Health	3 320	3 612	2 936	3 020
Trade and Industry	4 133	5 164	5 748	5 657
Not classified	1 462	1 560	2 406	0
TOTAL	199 380	213 256	210 835	205 399

– Data not available.
1.   Including State enterprises (such as Post and Telecommunications, State Railways and Bank of Finland).
2.   Excluding military conscripts.
3.   Includes universities (21 390 persons in 1992) and some professional institutions of education and culture.
4.   Including police administration and border patrol.
5.   Including judges and judiciary personnel.
Source: Tietoja valtion henkilöstöstä 1970-1992 (Facts about central government personnel, No. 20), the State Employer's Office, Ministry of Finance.

Table 3.   **State sector[1] personnel by type of institution**

	1980	1985	1991	1992
Ministries	3 873	4 833	5 466	5 318
Central agencies	7 778	7 934	6 887	6 160
Other central bodies[2]	101 539	104 099	38 223	38 192
Counties	2 153	1 969	2 106	2 104
District sectoral authorities[3]	56 512	60 159	57 967	51 388
Local sectoral units[4]	26 063	30 558	32 822	41 938
State enterprises	–	–	64 958	60 299
Not classified	1 462	3 704	2 406	–
TOTAL	199 380	213 256	210 835	205 399

– Data not available.
1.   Including State enterprises.
2.   Organisations at central level, many of which have become "unincorporated State enterprises" in 1989.
3.   Agencies at regional level such as county, provincial courts, military districts, customs districts, county taxation agencies, fishery districts).
4.   *E.g.* local police, tax offices, and unemployment offices.
Source: Tietoja valtion henkilöstöstä 1970-1992 (Facts about central government personnel, No. 20), the State Employer's Office, Ministry of Finance.

Table 4. **State sector[1] personnel by function[2]**

	1980	1985	1991	1992
Public administration	21 435	24 081	25 573	23 935
Public order and safety	20 960	22 729	23 509	22 502
Defence	20 390	22 382	21 338	20 044
Education, science and culture	21 287	28 389	35 819	33 683
Social security	1 475	1 824	1 460	2 009
Health services	1 845	1 788	1 476	1 500
Housing and environment	4 577	5 273	5 458	5 064
Labour	2 929	3 263	4 381	12 611
Agriculture and forestry	4 441	5 283	5 779	4 892
Communication and transport	94 051	88 900	77 246	70 358
Manufacturing and other industry	4 528	5 640	6 390	6 059
Other	–	–	–	140
TOTAL STATE	199 380	213 256	210 835	205 399
State enterprises	*76 937*	*71 956*	*64 958*	*60 299*
State administration	*122 443*	*141 300*	*145 877*	*145 100*

– Data not available.
1.   Including State enterprises.
2.   Classification of functions used by the budget administration.
Source: Tietoja valtion henkilöstöstä 1970-1992 (Facts about central government personnel, No. 20), the State Employer's Office, Ministry of Finance.

Table 5. **Employment by level of government**

	1980	1985	1991	1992
State administration	123 443	141 300	145 877	145 100
Municipalities[1]	337 000	427 000	458 000	448 000
TOTAL GOVERNMENT[1]	460 443	568 300	603 877	593 100
State enterprises	76 937	71 956	64 958	60 299
TOTAL PUBLIC SECTOR	537 380	640 256	668 835	653 399

1.   Including municipal public enterprises.
Source: For State data: Tietoja valtion henkilöstöstä 1970-1992 (Facts about central government personnel, No. 20), the State Employer's Office, Ministry of Finance. For municipal data: The Municipal Employers office.

Table 6. **Employment by industry and employer sector**
(in thousands)

	1985	1990	1991	1992
Public sector	674	705	709	684
State Sector	*226*	*226*	*222*	*220*
Local Sector	*447*	*479*	*487*	*464*
Public Administration and Defence	–	129	–	122

– Data not available.
Source: Statistics Finland Labour Force Statistics.

FRANCE

Introduction

In the following Tables 1 to 4, the public sector is broken down in 4 components: the State public administration, the territorial public administration, the hospital public administration and the national public institutions and public operations (*"exploitants publics"*).

Figures for the State administration, for national public institutions and public operations are provided by the national statistical office INSEE and are based on pay records and on surveys by the INSEE and by the General Directorate for Administration and the Public Service.

Figures for the territorial administration are provided by annual surveys carried out by INSEE.

Figures for hospital administration are provided through surveys undertaken by the Ministry of Social Affairs (Directorate for Hospitals, Statistical Service).

A regrouping of the data for the whole public sector has been done for the period 1945-1989 in *"Annales statistiques de la fonction publique, INSEE-Résultats n° 28-29"*.

Table 5 is based on the classification of economic units by institutional sector provided for by the *"Système élargi de la comptabilité nationale (SECN)"*. The SECN is the French equivalent of the system of national accounts (SNA) of the United Nations. The French concept of *"administrations publiques"* corresponds thus to the SNA concept of general government.

Table 1. **Personnel in State civil service (ministries) (excluding public institutions)**

(in thousands on 31 December)

	1980	1985	1991	1992[1]
National Education, Youth and Sport[2]	1 001.1	1 058.0	1 105.3	1 119.8
Post and Telecommunications[3]	482.0	514.0	0.8	0.8
Defence[4]	453.9	449.1	412.6[5]	412.6[5]
Economic Affairs and Finance	198.1	208.0	202.6	207.6
Interior, Overseas departments and Territories	139.0	151.1	160.0	164.8
Public facilities, Housing, Transportation and Maritime Affairs	112.1	114.7	123.7	124.0
Justice	42.3	49.0	57.5	58.3
Agriculture	34.6	34.9	36.5	35.2
Health, Labour	26.8	26.3	23.9	25.1
Foreign Affairs, Co-operation	35.5	29.9	23.9[5]	26.2
Culture	8.6	12.2	13.2	13.1
Industry, Research, Trade	5.8	10.3	13.2	14.9
Prime Ministry, Veterans	10.2	8.9	6.9	6.4
TOTAL	2 550.0	2 666.4	2 179.3[6]	2 208.8

1. Provisional.
2. Including teachers – up to and including university level – for public education (excluding private education teachers paid by the State).
3. A reorganisation of the post and telecommunications sector on 1.1.91 created 2 public enterprises known as "exploitants publics" ("La Poste" and "France Télécom"). Their staff ceased to be considered as State civil servants from that date. The Ministry of Post and Telecommunications (494 000 staff in 1990) had a workforce of about 800 until 1993.
4. Including military personnel (career staff).
5. Figures for 1990.
6. Staff reduction related to exclusion of Post and Telecommunications.
Source: Recensement des agents de l'État, INSEE/DGAFP.

Table 2. **Personnel in territorial and hospital administrations**

(in thousands on 31 December)

	1980	1985	1991
Local administration:	1 021.0	1 185.2	1 350.3
Regions	*0.3*	*2.9*	*5.9*
Departments	*133.7*	*155.0*	*184.7*
Municipalities	*754.9*	*862.8*	*954.3*
Intermunicipal bodies	*61.0*	*81.2*	*86.6*
Other bodies[1]	*71.1*	*83.3*	*118.8*
Hospital administration:	701.7	786.7	828.2
Including medical personnel	*82.7*	*101.4*	*109.6*
TOTAL	1 722.7	1 971.9	2 178.5

1. Including various private and semi-public administrative bodies, various ''industrial and commercial'' public bodies, trade unions, private bodies for local action, public HLM offices (controlled rent housing), municipal credit banks.
Source: For 1980 and 1985: Annales statistiques de la fonction publique, INSEE-Résultats No. 28-29.
    For 1991: Fonction publique territoriale: Enquête annuelle sur les effectifs des collectivités territoriales, INSEE Première No. 250.
    Fonction publique hospitalière: Ministère des Affaires sociales (SESI and Direction des hôpitaux).

Table 3. **Personnel in national public institutions and ''exploitants publics''**

(in thousands on 31 December)

	1980	1984	1988	1990
National public institutions having a public administration function[1]	169.8	188.1	183.7	188.5
Public enterprises with public institution status[2]	539.2	543.8	481.5	428.3
''Exploitants publics''[3]				494.9
TOTAL	709.0	731.9	665.2	1 111.7

1. Examples: CNRS, Commissariat à l'énergie atomique, ANPE, CROUS, etc. This category includes here the institutions which the extended National Accounting System (French equivalent of the SNA) does not classify as public administration, *i.e.* the CDC, CCCE, and ONF (totalling 20 505 staff in 1990).
2. Examples: Aéroports de Paris, Charbonnages de France, EDF/GDF, RATP, SNCF, etc.
3. La Poste and France Télécom: see note 3, Table 1.
Source: Annales statistiques de la fonction publique, INSEE Résultats No. 28-29.

Table 4. **Total public sector personnel**

(in thousands on 31 December)

	1980	1985	1991
State adminsitration	2 550.0	2 666.4	2 179.3
Territorial and hospital administration	1 722.7	1 971.9	2 178.5
National public institutions and ''exploitants publics''	709.0	731.9[1]	1 111.7[2]
TOTAL	4 981.7	5 370.2	5 469.5

1. Figure for 1984.
2. Figure for 1990.

Table 5. **Total public sector personnel**

(in thousands)

	1985	1991	1992
Central government administration	2 756.8	2 844.7	2 819.6
Local government administration	1 143.1	1 254.6	1 292.8
Social security administration	1 056.0	1 089.9	1 111.2
TOTAL	4 955.9	5 189.2	5 223.6

Source: Rapport sur les Comptes de la Nation 1992, INSEE Résultats.

GERMANY

Introduction

The tables have been prepared on the basis of figures provided by the Federal Statistical Office, but correspond to two different sources which are not comparable. In Table 1 the public sector is made up of the public service *(Offentliger Dienst)* plus legally autonomous institutions and enterprises which are, however, mainly financed by the government authority. The tables below provide data only on the public service.

The public service is divided into the direct *(Unmittelbar)* and the indirect *(Mittelbar)* public service. The direct public service includes personnel employed directly by a federal land or communal administration. It comprises public authorities at the three levels of government (including the judiciary) and legally non-autonomous institutions (such as hospitals, universities and schools) and enterprises directly administered by the government authority. It also includes German Railways, German Post and Telecommunications. The indirect public service includes personnel employed by a Federal or Land Corporation under public law such as the Federal Employment Office and social security organisations.

Table 2 also provided by the Federal Statistical Office is a statistic of employees based on administrative records of the Federal Employment Office. Only employees subject to compulsory social security are recorded. As such the self-employed and civil servants are excluded. The notion of ''government sector'' is based on an industrial classification *(Verzeichnis der Wirtschafzweige)* and is composed of public administration *(Gebietskörperschaften)* and social security.

Table 1.1. **Public service employment in Germany**[1]

(30 June, in thousands, head count, full-time and part-time)

	1991	1992
Direct public service:	6 412.6	6 305.0
Federation[2,3]	*652.0*	*624.7*
Länder[3]	*2 572.0*	*2 531.3*
Communes	*1 995.9*	*2 015.2*
Intercommunal associations	*55.5*	*58.3*
German Railways	*473.8*	*433.9*
German Post and Telecommunications	*663.5*	*641.5*
Indirect public service	325.1	352.2
TOTAL	6 737.8	6 657.2

1.   Sum of former Federal Republic, new *Länder* and East Berlin.
2.   Including military conscripts (257.3 in 1991 and 245.8 in 1992).
3.   Including police.
Source: Statistisches Bundesamt.

Table 1.2.   **Public service employment in the former Federal Republic**

(30 June, in thousands, head count, full-time and part-time)

	1991	1992
Direct public service:	4 680.0	4 684.5
Federation[1,2]	*567.1*	*544.0*
Länder[2]	*1 937.5*	*1 947.5*
Communes	*1 334.4*	*1 360.5*
Intercommunal associations	*55.1*	*57.1*
Germany Railways	*243.3*	*238.0*
German Post and Telecommunications	*542.6*	*537.4*
Indirect public service	277.3	287.7
TOTAL	4 957.3	4 972.2

1.   Including military conscripts (239.3 in 1991 and 222.5 in 1992).
2.   Including police.
Source: Statistisches Bundesamt.

Table 1.3.   **Public service employment in the new *Länder* and East Berlin**

(30 June, in thousands, head count, full-time and part-time)

	1991	1992
Direct public service:	1 732.1	1 620.5
Federation[1,2]	*84.9*	*80.7*
Länder[2]	*634.5*	*583.8*
Communes	*661.5*	*654.7*
Intercommunal associations	*0.5*	*1.2*
Germany Railways	*230.5*	*195.9*
German Post and Telecommunications	*120.7*	*104.1*
Indirect public service	47.9	64.5
TOTAL	1 780.5	1 685.0

1.   Including military conscripts (17.9 in 1991 and 23.4 in 1992).
2.   Including police.
Source: Statistisches Bundesamt.

Table 2.   **Employees[1] in Public administration and social security organisations[2]**

(30 June, in thousands, number of persons)

	1989	1990	1991	1992
Public administration	–	–	1 270.8	1 271.0
Social security	–	–	199.3	209.7
TOTAL	1 443.1	1 454.5	1 470.1	1 480.7

– = Not available.
1.   Employees submitted to compulsory social security, excluding notably civil servants.
2.   *Gebietskörperschaften und Sozialversicherung* from the industrial classification.
Source: Statistisches Bundesamt "Bevölkerung und Erwerbstätigkeit" *fachserie 1. Reihe 4.2.1. Struktur der Arbeitnehmer,* 30 June 1992.

GREECE

Table 1. **Public service employment in ministries**

(at 31 December each year)

	1990	1991	1992	1993
Presidency of Government	1 565	1 664	1 544	1 506
Aegean	85	82	85	91
Agriculture	15 531	15 007	15 065	14 780
Commerce	1 566	1 310	1 271	1 258
Culture	5 653	6 158	5 149	5 171
Defence	21 610	20 983	19 400	18 576
Environment, Urban Development and Public Works	9 625	9 512	9 169	9 033
Finance	18 805	19 185	20 480	20 519
Foreign Affairs	2 279	2 418	2 378	2 475
Health and Social Security	6 337	6 529	5 892	11 539
Industry, Energy and Technology	988	966	746	744
Interior	2 986	2 870	2 780	2 807
Justice [1]	12 198	12 493	11 999	12 112
Labour	854	846	862	881
Macedonia and Thrace	106	105	114	117
Merchant Navy	396	372	467	450
National Economy	2 193	2 855	2 276	2 237
National Education and Religion [2]	120 889	123 264	121 713	124 252
Public Order	6 129	5 651	5 379	5 253
Tourism	9	–	–	–
Transport and Communications	1 754	1 736	1 740	1 767
TOTAL	231 558	234 006	228 509	235 568

– Data not available.
1. Including judges.
2. Including teachers.
Source: Electronic Data Processing Division, Ministry to the Presidency of Government.

Table 2. **Public sector personnel by type of institution**

(at 31 December each year)

	1990	1991	1992	1993
Ministries	231 558	234 006	232 509	235 768
Public establishments	89 230	84 234	85 361	86 712
Local authorities	39 995	41 078	41 575	42 129
Public enterprises	137 500	133 565	115 867	113 321
Public Enterprise Rehabilitation Board	21 899	13 644	4 163	3 932
TOTAL	520 182	506 527	479 475	481 862

Source: Electronic Data Processing Division, Ministry to the Presidency of Government.

ICELAND

Table 1. **Government employment**

(in full-time equivalents)

	1980	1985	1989	1990	1991
Producers of government services [1]	16 605	19 911	22 221	23 000	23 082

1.   As defined in the System of National Accounts.
Source: National Accounts, Vol. II: Detailed Tables 1979-1991, OECD, Paris, 1993.

IRELAND

Introduction

The two tables below are both provided by the Department of Finance. The concept of the public service is in alignment with the SNA concept of general government. It includes the following elements:

- civil servants (also referred to as non-industrial staff) and state industrial employees from the departments and offices of the State and from local authorities, offices are generally independent of ministerial and departmental control in the execution of their functions;
- the President's Establishment, Parliament and judiciary;
- police and defence forces (voluntary military service);
- education: all teaching and non-teaching staff in primary, secondary and higher education and in vocational education funded (partially) by the State or local authorities;
- health services (including health boards and voluntary hospitals);
- non-commercial State bodies dependent upon the State for financial support and controlled by the State (the boards of directors are ministerial appointees). Typical such bodies are engaged in promotional, development, research and training activities.

The notion of the public sector consists of the government sector plus commercial State bodies including *inter alia* national electricity, telecommunications, postal, airline, and television/radio companies. The Central Statistical Office uses the same definition apart from the non-inclusion of the President's Establishment, Parliament and the judiciary.

Table 1. **Civil servants by department and office**

(full-time equivalents)

	July 1981	January 1985	January 1991	January 1994
Agriculture, Food, Fisheries	5 167	4 548	3 624	3 773.5
Arts, Culture, *Gaeltacht*	295	265	244	286.5
Attorney	22	24	32	35
Central Statistical Office	651	465	473	622.5
Chief State Solicitor's Office	93	83	114	134
Civil Service Commission	223	138	104	92
Comptroller	96	85	79	82
Defence	699	605	436	438
Director of Public Prosecutions	16	16	16	24.5
Education	1 011	933	821	815.5
Enterprise and Employment	1 570	1 419	1 007	945
Environment	1 096	939	789	798.5
Equality and Law Reform	88	82	62	75
Finance	900	778	550	531.5
Foreign Affairs	803	759	774	793
Health	400	354	335	383
Justice	3 958	3 990	4 633	5 106
Marine	283	259	308	356.5
National Gallery	17	17	12	14
Office of Public Works	1 260	1 128	821	833
Oireachtas (Parliament)	191	202	196	225
Ombudsman	0	19	34	32
Ordnance Survey	394	363	298	287
President's Establishment	10	10	10	13
Revenue	7 215	6 818	6 017.5	6 009.5
Social Welfare	3 335	3 410	3 778	4 257
State Laboratory	62	65	61	73
Tanaiste (Deputy Prime Minister)	0	0	0	20
Taoiseach (Prime Minister)	160	139	129	138
Tourism and Trade	107	93	75	98
Transport, Energy, Communications	822	767	620	634
Valuation Office	209	190	149	157.5
TOTAL	31 153	28 963	26 601.5	28 083

Source: Department of Finance.

Table 2.   **Public service and public sector employment**
(as at 1 January, full-time equivalents)

	1980	1981	1987	1988	1989	1990	1991	1992	1993	1994 (estimate)
Civil Service	33 794	34 673	30 993	31 404	28 312	28 003	28 536	29 226	29 813	29 947
Non-industrial	*30 635*	*31 153*	*28 445*	*28 236*	*26 304*	*26 015*	*26 602*	*27 302*	*27 957*	*28 083*
Temp. Clerical trainees	*0*	*0*	*100*	*700*	*0*	*0*	*0*	*0*	*0*	*0*
Industrial	*3 159*	*3 520*	*2 448*	*2 468*	*2 008*	*1 988*	*1 934*	*1 924*	*1 856*	*1 864*
Garda Siochana (National Police)	9 600	9 882	11 477	11 198	10 828	10 900	11 234	11 303	11 463	11 468
Gardai	–	*9 870*	*11 382*	*11 109*	*10 749*	*10 472*	*10 601*	*10 786*	*10 984*	*10 895*
Recruits	–	–	–	–	–	*346*	*536*	*413*	*357*	*453*
Traffic wardens	–	*12*	*95*	*89*	*79*	*82*	*97*	*104*	*122*	*120*
Defence Forces	15 500	16 365	15 340	14 791	14 818	14 387	14 761	14 564	14 361	14 090
Military	–	*14 314*	*13 728*	*13 249*	*13 348*	*12 927*	*13 311*	*13 119*	*12 951*	*12 740*
Civilian Employees	–	*2 051*	*1 612*	*1 542*	*1 470*	*1 460*	*1 450*	*1 445*	*1 410*	*1 350*
Education	49 100	51 000	54 500	54 403	51 992	51 306	51 666	52 910	54 466	55 821
Non-commercial State bodies	6 900	8 760	9 148	8 785	7 777	7 131	7 119	7 963	7 993	8 121
Health Services	59 486	66 197	61 557	56 991	55 295	57 239	58 743	59 497	60 566	61 839
Local Authorities	31 728	32 505	32 383	30 252	26 892	26 468	26 697	26 715	26 793	27 000
Officers	*8 796*	*8 767*	*9 956*	*9 435*	*8 728*	*8 759*	*8 939*	*9 098*	*9 217*	*9 424*
Servants	*22 932*	*23 738*	*22 427*	*20 817*	*18 164*	*17 709*	*17 742*	*17 617*	*17 576*	*17 576*
TOTAL PUBLIC SERVICE	206 108	219 382	215 398	207 824	195 914	195 524	198 756	202 178	205 455	208 286
Commercial State Bodies	90 375	91 001	78 995	73 864	72 516	71 931	71 874	66 654	64 590	63 560
TOTAL PUBLIC SECTOR	296 483	310 383	294 393	281 688	268 430	267 455	270 630	268 832	270 045	271 846

– = Not available.
Source: Department of Finance.

ITALY

Table 1.　Personnel in Ministries

Structure of the public sector	1980	1985	1988	1992
Presidency of the Council of Ministers	3 630	4 390	5 215	6 382
Agriculture and Forestry	4 739	4 051	3 877	3 043
Forestry workers	*4 579*	*4 930*	*5 424*	*6 880*
Budget and Economic Planning	248	229	249	323
Cultural Heritage	13 551	24 095	26 148	24 431
Defence	46 030	54 593	52 915	53 928
Military staff	*175 627*	*193 940*	*210 848*	*220 517*
Education	9 021	9 872	12 240	11 386
Teachers	*965 459*	*1 053 863*	*1 068 358*	*1 073 465*
Employment and Social Security	11 350	16 935	15 508	15 380
Environment	0	0	79	164
Finance	57 339	69 404	66 721	68 238
Financial police	*44 895*	*48 167*	*53 813*	*58 388*
Foreign Affairs	4 418	4 870	5 023	5 051
Foreign Trade	497	505	541	528
Health	2 223	4 826	5 144	4 900
Industry, Trade and Handicrafts	1 382	1 437	1 457	1 431
Interior	9 882	12 455	17 103	20 739
National police	*70 342*	*75 535*	*80 664*	*95 814*
Fire brigade	*15 694*	*17 708*	*23 544*	*25 257*
Justice	32 618	39 801	42 971	48 781
Prison officers	*16 735*	*22 021*	*23 160*	*28 805*
Merchant Navy	1 143	1 489	1 631	3 725
Post and Telecommunications	0	0	0	0
Public Works	5 012	4 720	4 372	4 361
State Industrial Holdings	147	139	129	120
Tourism	326	304	377	422
Transport	3 722	5 509	5 635	6 531
Treasury	12 385	13 796	15 748	17 904
Universities and Scientific and Technological Research	0	0	0	0
Universities	63 660	81 043	89 197	100 677
TOTAL	1 576 654	1 770 627	1 838 091	1 907 571

Source: Ministero del Tesoro, Ragionera Generale dello Stato.

Table 2. **Public Sector Personnel**

	1985	1988	1990	1992
Ministries[1]	272 188	275 476	289 795	291 302
Non-commercial public organisations[2]	80 790	81 353	77 739	76 641
Local authorities[3]	697 768	725 253	798 228	728 686
Autonomous bodies	301 760	303 019	298 672	292 785
Local health units	691 954	657 645	645 591	657 435
Research establishments	19 820	16 794	17 384	16 854
Schools	1 040 203	1 077 893	1 061 184	1 070 055
Universities[4]	90 752	90 836	107 708	108 870
Armed forces	273 616	293 958	305 493	312 606
Military corps	80 936	89 858	97 658	131 499
TOTAL	3 549 787	3 612 085	3 699 452	3 686 733

1. Including magistrates, managers, posts to be suppressed, municipal and provincial secretaries.
2. Including managers.
3. Including salaried personnel of regions with special status and of the autonomous provinces of Trento and Balzano.
4. Including university professors, managers, and posts to be suppressed.
Source: Department of the Public Service.

JAPAN

Table 1. **National government employees by ministry**

(fiscal years and fixed numbers)

	1980	1985	1992	1993
NON-INDUSTRIAL				
Cabinet	190	194	249	249
Prime Minister's Office:	57 543	55 387	53 174	52 967
Office proper [1]	*3 373*	*609*	*588*	*591*
Fair Trade Commission	*422*	*432*	*484*	*493*
National Public Safety Commission	*8 180*	*8 140*	*8 203*	*8 212*
Environmental Disputes Coordination Commission	*40*	*40*	*40*	*40*
Imperial Household Agency	*1 144*	*1 129*	*1 124*	*1 135*
Management and Coordination Agency [1]	*1 480*	*3 989*	*3 735*	*3 703*
Hokkaido Development Agency	*10 109*	*9 114*	*8 214*	*8 126*
Defense Agency	*27 640*	*26 783*	*25 616*	*25 473*
Economic Planning Agency	*522*	*505*	*508*	*510*
Science and Technology Agency	*2 179*	*2 145*	*2 119*	*2 121*
Environment Agency	*895*	*903*	*937*	*955*
Okinawa Development Agency	*1 108*	*1 146*	*1 148*	*1 149*
National Land Agency	*451*	*452*	*458*	*459*
Justice	49 938	49 911	50 447	50 646
Foreign Affairs	3 480	3 883	4 522	4 636
Finance	68 280	67 673	70 884	71 431
Education	130 460	136 416	137 567	137 765
Health and Welfare	74 363	74 633	75 558	75 728
Agriculture, Forestry and Fisheries	50 162	45 415	38 896	38 252
International Trade and Industry [2]	*12 796*	*12 672*	*12 365*	*12 376*
Transport	38 180	37 679	37 564	37 674
Posts and Telecommunications	3 002	2 902	2 799	2 798
Labour	25 518	24 968	24 878	24 875
Construction	28 638	26 487	24 490	24 322
Home Affairs	555	544	571	573
TOTAL NON-INDUSTRIAL	543 105	538 764	533 964	534 292
INDUSTRIAL				
Mint	1 719	1 628	1 531	1 517
Printing	6 832	6 564	6 211	6 166
National forestry	33 068	27 520	16 041	14 406
Alcohol [2]	943	–	–	–
Postal service	312 699	310 225	304 701	304 864
TOTAL INDUSTRIAL	355 261	345 937	328 484	326 953
TOTAL	898 366	884 701	862 448	861 245

1. The Management and Coordination Agency (MCA) was established and the Administrative Management Agency abolished in 1984. The MCA was made up of all the offices in the former AMA and most of the offices in the Prime Minister's Office proper.
2. The larger part of the National Industry of Alcohol was transformed into a public corporation and the other part joined the Ministry of International Trade and Industry (non-industrial) in 1981.
Source: Administrative Management Bureau, Management and Coordination Agency.

Table 2. **National government employees**

(fiscal years and fixed numbers)

	1980	1985	1992	1993
Ministries and Agencies	898 366	884 701	862 448	861 245
Self-defence officials	270 184	272 162	274 652	273 801
Ministers, Parliamentary Vice-Ministers, etc.	138	137	142	142
Diet	4 068	4 062	4 067	4 066
Courts	24 482	24 525	24 702	24 733
Board of Audit	1 224	1 229	1 240	1 243
National Personnel Authority	715	710	712	713
TOTAL	1 199 177	1 187 526	1 167 963	1 165 943

Source: Administrative Management Bureau, Management and Coordination Agency.

Table 3. **Local government employees**

(fiscal years and fixed numbers)

	1980	1985	1990	1992
General administration	1 068 784	1 056 895	1 055 116	1 072 826
Taxation	87 072	85 156	83 586	83 202
Educational	1 269 533	1 309 942	1 297 802	1 292 262
Medical	161 539	182 322	199 143	206 406
Police	240 335	246 067	250 513	252 506
Fire services	120 895	129 092	134 022	137 983
Other	88 742	87 758	88 535	90 382
Public enterprises	130 844	124 787	119 601	118 724
TOTAL	3 167 744	3 222 019	3 228 318	3 254 291

Source: Public Service Personnel Department, Local Administration Bureau, Ministry of Home Affairs.

Table 4. **Government employees by level**

(fiscal years and fixed numbers)

	1980	1985	1990	1993
National	1 199 177	1 187 526	1 171 763	1 165 943
Local (prefectures)	1 705 587	1 744 633	1 741 447	1 742 121 [1]
Local (cities, towns and villages)	1 462 157	1 477 386	1 486 871	1 512 170 [1]
TOTAL	4 366 921	4 409 545	4 400 081	4 420 234

1. 1992 fiscal year.
Sources: National: Administrative Management Bureau, Management and Coordination Agency.
    Local: Public Service Personnel Department, Local Administration Bureau, Ministry of Home Affairs.

LUXEMBOURG

Introduction

Table 1 below is based on data provided by the Administration of State Personnel of the Ministry for the Public Service. The Public administration is composed of: the central administration (ministries and general services), local administration (communes and communal associations) and State public institutions (*Institut Monétaire Luxebourgeois, Office des Assurances sociales etc.*).

The table relates only to civil servants from the central administration, and excludes state employees and workers. The rubric General Administration includes civil servants from Post and Telecommunications (approx. 1500 persons); as from from 1 January 1993 Post and Telecommunications became a public enterprise.

Table 2 is based on data provided by the Central Statistical Office (STATEC) which uses a standard industrial classification. These figures correspond with the SNA data published by the OECD.

Table 1. **Civil servants in central administration**

(fixed numbers)

	1970	1985	1990	1991	1992	1970-92 Growth	%
General administration	3 819	5 009	5 427	5 590	5 661	1 842	48.2
Magistracy	171	244	260	268	281	110	64.3
Armed forces[1]	1 011	1 136	1 262	1 297	1 335	324	32.0
Education[2]	2 558	3 801	4 410	4 486	4 612	2 054	80.3
Religion	364	225	228	227	227	−137	−37.6
Special functions	11	13	13	13	13	2	18.2
TOTAL	7 934	10 428	11 600	11 881	12 129	4 195	52.9

1.   Including non-military civil servants.
2.   Including non-teaching civil servants in National Education.
Source: Activity Report, Ministry of the Public Service.

Table 2. **Internal employment in activity branch "Producers of government services"**

	1980	1990	1991	1992[1]
Public administrations	17 100	20 700	21 400	21 800

1.   Estimate.
Source: STATEC.

NETHERLANDS

Introduction

The definition of the government sector used in the tables below provided by the Ministry of Home Affairs does not differ from the definition of ''general government'' as used in the Dutch national accounts and is consistent with the SNA concept. However, provinces, municipalities and intercommunal associations include employees of their public enterprises.

Table 1. **Persons employed in Ministries and Higher Courts of State**

(number of persons full-time and part-time)

	1980	1985	1991	1992	1993[4]
Higher Courts of State	–	1 374	1 633	1 732	1 701
Cabinet of Dutch Antilles and Aruban Affairs	–	57	49	65	80
Agriculture, Conservation of National Scenery and Fisheries	10 624	11 951	11 883	11 718	10 840
Defence (civilian employees)[1]	28 582	28 206	0	0	0
Economic Affairs	6 113	6 768	5 498	5 298	5 260
Education and Science	3 754	4 226	3 446	3 403	3 379
Finance	31 818	34 850	32 955	32 328	31 976
Foreign Affairs	1 686	1 721	3 198	3 242	3 269
General Affairs	401	384	392	391	370
Home Affairs[2]	4 074	3 282	2 489	2 354	2 376
Housing, Physical Planning and Environment	7 573	8 247	7 506	7 363	7 286
Justice[3]	16 760	19 244	18 764	19 145	20 313
Social Affairs and Employment	5 959	7 141	2 661	2 566	2 513
Transport and Public Works	20 412	19 900	15 838	15 606	14 447
Welfare, Health and Cultural Affairs	8 727	7 049	7 432	7 537	7 250
TOTAL	146 483	154 400	113 744	112 748	111 060

– Data not available.
1.   Civilian personnel of Ministry of Defence transferred to National Army in 1991.
2.   In 1980, includes Higher Courts of State.
3.   Administrative personnel of the State Police, transferred from the Ministry of Justice to the Police Force in 1991. (A similar transfer for the Municipal Police Force will take place in 1994.)
4.   Provisional figures.
Source: Directorate for Conditions of Work in the Public Sector (DGMP/AO), Ministry of Home Affairs, published in *Kerngegevens Bezoldiging en Personeel.*

Table 2. **Persons employed in the government sector**

(number of persons full-time and part-time)

	1980	1985	1991	1992	1993[5]
Central government Ministries and Higher Courts of State	146 483	154 400	113 744	112 748	111 060
Judiciary	1 409	1 277	1 583	1 873	1 967
Police force:	30 099	30 714	35 689	36 156	–
State police	–	–	*10 573*	*10 481*	*10 239*
Admininistrative personnel of State Police[1]	–	–	*4 806*	*4 644*	*4 103*
Municipal police	–	–	*20 310*	*21 031*	–
National army:	135 739	103 160	121 064	114 194	105 681
Conscripts	–	–	*45 673*	*40 617*	*33 032*
Civilian Personnel Ministry of Defence[2]	–	–	*24 088*	*23 573*	*22 306*
Military	–	–	*51 303*	*50 004*	*50 343*
Education:	243 248	304 782	302 929	331 080	363 423
Primary	–	–	*112 354*	*124 288*	–
Secondary	–	–	*108 022*	*121 514*	–
Agricultural	–	–	*3 004*	*2 454*	–
Higher vocational[3]	–	–	*26 492*	*27 508*	*28 811*
Universities	–	–	*53 057*	*55 316*	*55 764*
Municipalities[4]	210 969	214 806	196 017	187 329	–
Provinces[4]	17 002	18 357	13 951	14 176	–
Polder boards[3]	–	7 275	7 815	7 835	–
Intercommunal associations[3, 4]	–	–	21 222	21 393	–
TOTAL	784 949	834 771	814 014	826 784	–

– Data not available.
1. Administrative personnel of the State Police, transferred from the Ministry of Justice in 1991. (A similar transfer in the Municipal Police Force will take place in 1994.)
2. Civilian personnel of the Ministry of Defence transferred to the National Army in 1991.
3. Polder boards, intercommunal associations and higher vocational education have been added to the government sector since 1983, 1986 and 1991 respectively.
4. Figures for municipalities, provinces and intercommunal associations include employees of their public enterprises (such as transport and electricity supply).
5. Provisional figures.
Source: Directorate for Conditions of Work in the Public Sector (DGMP/AO), Ministry of Home Affairs, published in *Kerngegevens Bezoldiging en Personeel.*

NEW ZEALAND

Introduction

The tables below derive from two different sources. The Department of Statistics Quarterly Employment Survey figures (Table 2) are based on the New Zealand Standard Institutional Sector Classification (NZISC) which includes a "general government sector" concept similar to the SNA concept. General government is composed of central and local government non-trading activities, excluding the military. With the addition of public trading activities from the "producer enterprises" sector (namely government enterprises) and from the "financial intermediaries" sector (namely the Central Bank, and insurance and pension funds operated by central and local government), one obtains the "public sector". This source also uses a standard industrial classification (NZSIC convertible to ISIC) so that a cross-tabulation of general government employment by industrial class should be possible. It should be noted that several industry groups are excluded from the survey (mainly agriculture, fisheries and seagoing areas) which has currently only a small effect on the public sector. It had a more significant impact before NZ rail (Inter-Island Rail Ferries) was privatised.

Table 1. **Total public service employment**

(in full-time equivalents 1980/85 and head count 1993/94)

	March 1980	March 1985	March 1993	March 1994
Ministry of Agriculture and Fisheries	6 083	5 928	2 930	3 010
Audit New Zealand	291	444	379	299
Auditor General[1]	–	–	–	51
Ministry of Commerce	–	–	655	654
Department of Conservation	–	–	1 798	1 726
Crown Law Office	22	25	75	89
Ministry of Cultural Affairs	–	–	10	13
Customs Department	1 136	1 213	812	826
Ministry of Defence[2]	3 274	3 293	59	59
Ministry of Education[3]	2 188	2 053	535	469
Education Review Office	–	–	164	170
Ministry for the Environment	–	–	111	122
Ministry of Foreign Affairs and Trade[4]	599	602	626	616
Ministry of Forestry[5]	7 231	7 796	142	153
Government Superannuation Fund	–	–	65	59
Ministry of Health[6]	4 411	3 933	611	394
Ministry of Housing	–	–	151	158
Inland Revenue Department	3 507	4 150	5 972	5 879
Department of Internal Affairs	3 104	3 326	2 768	2 762
Department of Justice	4 082	4 762	7 859	9 183
Labour Department	1 777	2 370	1 854	1 767
Ministry of Maori Development[7]	1 256	1 148	387	246
National Library	–	–	564	480
Ministry of Pacific Island Affairs	–	–	47	44
Department of Prime Minister and Cabinet	56	55	121	118
Public Trust Office	673	578	491	484
Ministry of Research, Science and Technology	–	–	38	34
Serious Fraud Office	–	–	42	37
Social Welfare Department	4 441	6 071	7 338	7 311
State Services Commission	759	827	164	144
Department of Statistics	787	799	812	842
Department of Survey and Land Information[8]	2 995	2 905	983	999
Ministry of Transport	4 587	4 358	795	57
Treasury	513	489	369	387
Valuation	698	641	432	449
Ministry of Women's Affairs	–	–	43	37
Ministry of Youth Affairs	–	–	29	25
Other[9]	29 650	27 612	30	0
TOTAL	84 120	85 378	40 261	40 153

– Did not exist in that year.
1.   Prior to March 1994 the office of the Auditor General was included under Audit New Zealand.
2.   In 1980 and 1985, Department of Defence.
3.   In 1980 and 1985, Department of Education.
4.   In 1980 and 1985, Ministry of Foreign Affairs. In 1992, Ministry of External Relations and Trade.
5.   In 1980 and 1985, Forest Service.
6.   In 1980, 1985 and 1992, Department of Health.
7.   In 1980 and 1985, Department of Maori Affairs.
8.   In 1980 and 1985, Lands and Survey.
9.   Includes 30 residual staff at the Housing Corporation.
Source: State Services Commission.

Table 2. **General government and public sector employment** [1]

(number of filled jobs, February figures)

	1989	1990	1991	1992	1993
General government:	231 000	236 800	241 400	229 900	230 100
Central government non-trading	*206 400*	*205 500*	*209 300*	*206 200*	*206 300*
Local government non-trading	*24 600*	*31 300*	*32 100*	*23 700*	*23 800*
Central government trading	23 700	66 300	44 000	39 400	29 400
Local government trading	19 600	15 300	14 900	18 500	15 800
TOTAL PUBLIC SECTOR [2]	334 300	318 400	300 200	287 800	275 300

1. Military not included.
2. Figures may not add due to rounding.
Source: Quarterly Employment Statistics, Department of Statistics.

NORWAY

Introduction

Figures come from two different sources. Figures for employment in central State administration by ministry in Table 1 are provided by the Ministry of Government Administration from personnel registers. They include employees in public enterprises and military career personnel (thus excluding conscripts). Public enterprises are part of the State and their employees are civil servants. This concerns national railways, the postal service and telecommunications. In contrast, publicly owned enterprises are independent legal units and their employees are not civil servants.

The figures in Table 2 come from the National Accounts Statistics of Statistics Norway. The concept of government is fully compatible with the concept of "producers of government services" (or very closely related "general government") of the 1968 System of National Accounts (SNA). This concept excludes public enterprises but includes all military (including conscripts). A major revision of this system is being carried out by Statistics Norway to comply with the revised 1993 SNA.

Table 1.   **Personnel in central State administration, by ministry**[1]

(full-time equivalents at 1 October each year)

	1980	1985	1991	1992
Agriculture	4 133	5 193	4 896	4 991
Children and Family[2]	–	–	353	393
Church, Education and Science[3]	13 551	1 794	16 632	17 768
Culture[4]	–	12 575	693	769
Defence	24 851	25 254	25 576	24 505
Environment	923	1 259	1 602	1 705
Finance	9 226	9 269	9 338	9 280
Fisheries	1 685	2 108	1 967	1 983
Foreign Affairs	956	763	1 876	1 845
Health and Social Affairs	16 060	12 204	11 746	12 332
Industry	889	994	659	662
Justice	11 978	12 864	14 583	15 113
Labour and Government Administration[5]	1 561	1 618	4 929	5 432
Local Government[6]	3 333	3 626	1 721	1 764
Petroleum and Energy	2 466	2 697	2 367	724
Trade and Shipping	886	854	–	–
Transport and Communication[7]	67 825	69 183	66 286	64 506
Other	452	988	61	72
TOTAL	160 505	163 243	165 285	163 844

– Data not available.
1.   Since 1980, 98 per cent of the personnel are in agencies and directorates subordinated to each ministry.
2.   Did not exist in 1980 or 1985.
3.   In 1980 and 1985, Church and Education only.
4.   Did not exist in 1980. In 1985, Culture and Science.
5.   In 1980 and 1985, Consumer Affairs and Government Administration.
6.   In 1980 and 1985, Local Government and Labour.
7.   Includes employees in State Railways, Postal Service and Telecommunications service.
Source: Ministry of Government Administration.

Table 2. **Personnel in central and local government**

(number of persons full-time and part-time)

	1980	1985	1991
Central government services	134 800	140 400	149 000
In percentages: Defence	*39.0%*	*37.0%*	*37.0%*
Education and research	*16.0%*	*16.0%*	*17.0%*
Health	*6.5%*	*5.0%*	*4.5%*
Welfare	*0.5%*	*0.5%*	*0.5%*
Other	*39.0%*	*42.0%*	*41.0%*
Local government services	317 200	369 800	435 000
In percentages: Education and research	*28.0%*	*28.0%*	*25.0%*
Health	*33.0%*	*35.0%*	*36.0%*
Welfare	*23.0%*	*20.0%*	*23.0%*
Other	*16.0%*	*17.0%*	*16.0%*
TOTAL GENERAL GOVERNMENT	452 000	510 200	584 000

Source: National Accounts Statistics, Statistics Norway.

PORTUGAL

Introduction

The data in the following tables come from two different sources. Tables 1 and 2 are based on ministerial sources. They do not include the autonomous regions outside continental Portugal. Table 3 is provided by the National Institute for Statistics and includes the autonomous regions. Both sources exclude personnel in public enterprises.

Table 1. **Central administration staff numbers**

	1983	1986	1991	1992
Office of the President of the Republic	173	226	263	263
Assembly of the Republic	247	222	327	332
Presidency of the Council of Ministers	2 234	2 106	4 014	4 217
Ombudsman	53	52	56	75
MINISTRIES				
Agriculture	22 662	18 363	20 741	16 388
Education[1]	157 931	183 028	206 024	230 070
Employment and Social Security	4 916	23 120	27 319	27 319
Environment and Natural Resources	–	–	3 207	4 044
Finance	16 919	17 610	23 867	23 798
Foreign Affairs	1 204	1 497	1 698	1 315
Health	89 390	92 853	108 850	103 916
Industry, Trade, Energy	7 610	6 454	6 084	5 762
Internal Administration	2 909	736	992	60 725[2]
Justice	16 859	17 785	19 412	18 744
National Defence	–	–	–	89 727[3]
The Plan and Territorial Administration	–	6 702	5 828	4 667
Public Works, Transport and Communications	–	13 687	7 761	6 145
Quality of Life	913	–	–	–
Sea	6 274	–	2 842	4 813
Social Services	14 134	–	–	–
TOTAL	344 428	384 441	439 285	602 320[4]

– Data not available.
1.   Including teaching personnel.
2.   Including security forces.
3.   Including military personnel.
4.   Substantial increase in 1992 mostly due to inclusion of military and security forces.
Sources: General Directorate for Public Administration; General Directorate for Public Accounting.

Table 2.　**Breakdown of personnel by level of administration**[1]

	1983	1986	1991	1992
Central administration[2]	344 428	384 441	439 285	602 320
Local administration	75 876	79 873	82 000	87 000
TOTAL	420 304	464 314	521 285	689 320

1.　Excluding autonomous regions.
2.　Excluding national defence, except in 1992.
Sources: General Directorate for Public Administration; General Directorate for Public Accounting; General Directorate for Local Administration.

Table 3.　**Employment in the public sector**[1]

	1989	1990[2]	1991[2]	1992[2]	1993[2]
TOTAL PUBLIC SECTOR	676 500	686 000	695 600	705 300	715 200

1.　This source covers central and local administration including autonomous regions. Military personnel and security forces are included. An estimate of the number of individuals currently doing compulsory military service has been made to comply with the SNA concept.
2.　1990-1993 data are estimates based on the annual average growth rate provided by the General Directorate for Public Administration.
Source: Instituto Nacional de Estatistica (INE).

SPAIN

Introduction

The data belong to two different sources. Tables 1 to 3 are based on administrative records (essentially the central personnel register of the Ministry for Public Administration). The concept used is public administration including teachers in public institutions, the judicial administration and the armed forces and excluding public enterprises. Table 4 is based on data provided by the national statistical office (INE) from the quarterly labour force survey. This survey uses a standard industrial classification (by branch of activity) which is convertible to the "International Standard Industrial Classification of all economic activities" (ISIC) and which contains the concept of "public administration, defence and compulsory social security". The survey retains also the notion of the public sector which comprises public enterprises (more then 50% of the capital equity is owned by the State), but excludes military conscripts.

Table 1. **Employment in Ministries**

	July 1991	November 1992	November 1993	February 1994
State administrations	3 047	3 134	2 630	2 645
Foreign Affairs	5 430	5 480	5 598	5 557
Social Affairs	8 538	8 599	11 548	11 597
Agriculture, Fishing and Food	14 983	13 665	11 561	11 407
Culture	4 805	4 826	5 032	5 118
Defence[1]	7 530	7 431	7 546	7 596
Economy and Finance	45 418	46 816	46 320	44 795
Education and science	229 090	224 467	229 037	236 259
of which: Teachers	*182 996*	*176 887*	*180 039*	*187 602*
Labour and Social Security[2]	56 269	59 076	59 382	59 211
Industry, Commerce and Tourism, Energy[3]	6 387	6 547	6 404	6 443
Interior[4]	14 760	14 989	15 227	15 364
Justice[5]	15 314	15 660	16 591	16 653
Presidency (Government spokesman, Relations with Parliament)[6]	3 602	3 717	3 890	3 897
Health and Consumer Protection[2]	9 387	9 240	8 908	8 663
Public Works, Transport and Environment	84 471	89 386	75 505[7]	74 758
of which: Post and Telecommunications	*55 737*	*56 574*	*52 335*	*51 830*
TOTAL	509 031	513 033	505 449	509 963

1. Excluding military and contract staff.
2. Excluding Social Security statutory personnel and health institutions personnel.
3. In 1993, the Ministry of Industry, Trade and Tourism has split up into Ministry of Industry and Energy and Ministry of Trade and Tourism.
4. Excluding State Security forces and personnel.
5. Excluding Justice Administration personnel. Includes ministry and penitentiary institutions personnel.
6. In 1993, the Ministry of Relations with Parliament and the Government Spokesman have been integrated into a new Ministry of the Presidency.
7. The decline is explained by the creation of two public enterprises (AENA and Puertos del Estado) whose personnel were included in the Ministry personnel.
Source: Central Personnel Registry, Ministry for Public Administration.

Table 2. **Employees in the central administration**

	November 1992	November 1993	February 1994
Employees in ministries:	513 033	505 449	509 963
Civil servants	*212 266*	*206 054*	*205 312*
Contract personnel[1]	*102 568*	*97 484*	*95 010*
Non-university teachers	*127 413*	*128 323*	*135 277*
University teaching and non-teaching personnel	*70 786*	*73 588*	*74 364*
State security forces and corps[2]	118 745	115 369	120 192
Armed forces	74 690	70 589	71 395
Employees for defence	36 866	37 465	36 718
Personnel in health institutions[3]	125 888	137 806	137 806
Justice administration personnel	35 007	37 318	37 347
TOTAL STATE ADMINISTRATION	904 229	903 996	913 421

1. Except in defence and health institutions.
2. Guardia Civil and Police.
3. Excluding personnel of Table 1.
Source: Central Personnel Registry, Ministry for Public Administration for employees in ministries; other ministerial sources for non-ministerial staff.

Table 3. **Employees by level of administration**

	November 1992	(%)	November 1993	(%)	February 1994	(%)
Central administration	904 229	(48)	903 996	(48)	913 421	(48)
Autonomous communities	593 453	(32)	612 374	(33)	612 374	(32)
Local administration	366 563	(20)	367 050	(19)	367 032	(19)
TOTAL	1 864 245	(100)	1 883 420	(100)	1 892 827	(100)

Source: Central Personnel Registry , Ministry for Public Administration.

Table 4. **Salaried employees by industrial branch and by sector**

(Third quarter 1993)

	Public Sector	Private Sector	Total	(Per cent of salaried employment)
Public administration, defense and compulsory social security	765 500	4 300	769 800	(8.8)
Education	422 600	152 500	575 000	(6.6)
Sanitary, veterinary activities, and social activities	419 600	139 900	559 500	(6.4)
Other activities and social services to the Community and personnel services	68 000	201 600	269 600	(3.1)
Other branches	452 400	6 085 800	6 538 200	(75.0)
TOTAL	2 128 100	6 584 100	8 712 200	(100.0)
(Per cent)	(24)	(76)	(100)	

Source: Labour Force Survey, National Institute of Statistics.

Table 5. Public sector salaried employees by type of administration
(Third quarter 1993)

	Employees	Percentage
Central administration	561 400	26.4
Autonomous Communities	500 000	23.5
Local administration	389 800	18.3
Social security	325 500	15.3
Public enterprises and institutions	347 100	16.3
Other (non classified)	4 300	0.2
TOTAL PUBLIC SECTOR	2 128 100	100.0

Source: Labour Force Survey, National Institute of Statistics.

SWEDEN

Introduction

The tables below are come from two different sources. Table 1 comes from the Ministry of Finance and concerns only civil servants and defence personnel (civilian and military but excepting conscripts) employed in the central administration. It excludes notably and principally employees in the public utilities (also called State business enterprises, *Affärsverken*). Table 2 is provided by the Statistical Office. The government sector in this source is broken down into central government, county councils, local authorities, and the Church of Sweden. These breakdowns are composed as follows:

– Central government (approximately one-quarter of the government sector):
   a) central government authorities, civilian and military (except conscripts), police, prison personnel, high schools and universities, the Parliament and courts of justice;
   b) State business enterprises: there are seven: postal service, railways, telecommunications, hydraulic power stations, National Forestry administration, Civil Aviation Authority and the maritime administration;
   c) other State regulated activity: essentially public insurance schemes, museums and research institutions;
– County councils (approximately one-quarter of the government sector): includes the county administration but is made up for the most part of health care institutions.
– Local authorities (slightly less than half of the government sector): municipal administration, but essentially social welfare and primary and gymnasium schools.
– Church of Sweden (one percent of the government sector).

The government sector does not include several hundred publicly owned companies *(Statliga och kommunal företage)* which operate in competition with the private sector (for example, forestry, pulp and paper factories).

Table 1.   **Personnel in central State administration by ministry** [1]

(number of persons full-time and part-time)

	1980	1985	1991	1992	1993
Central services for the ministries	–	–	320	340	340
Agriculture	8 049	14 404	10 480	10 530	9 970
Defence [2]	49 044	49 449	47 620	46 080	44 490
Education	50 030	55 727	48 590	46 420	47 480
Environment and Natural Resources	–	–	1 210	4 600	4 510
Finance	8 300	17 683	22 790	26 460	25 340
Foreign Affairs [3]	8 921	2 823	3 000	2 910	2 790
Health and Social Affairs	14 693	4 261	2 970	2 790	2 350
Housing [4]	4 533	4 428	4 780	–	–
Industry and Commerce	2 580	2 717	2 440	2 790	2 270
Justice [5]	43 259	44 956	17 320	44 540	44 670
Labour	16 280	17 583	23 090	21 070	16 110
Public Administration	23 100	18 383	38 890	7 270	6 770
Transport and Communication	9 500	14 384	18 380	18 360	18 230
TOTAL	238 289	246 798	241 880	234 160	225 520

– Figures not available.
1.   98 per cent of total employment is with agencies and boards attached to the ministries.
2.   Excluding conscripts.
3.   Including embassies, consulates, etc.
4.   Closed down in 1992.
5.   Including the Cabinet Office.
Source: Ministry of Finance.

Table 2.   **Personnel in the government sector by level and function**

(number of persons full-time and part-time)

	1980	1985	1991
Central government	427 300	423 100	395 000
In percentages: Management of the public sector	17.0%	17.3%	12.9%
Social welfare	2.2%	1.9%	1.9%
Health	2.2%	0.3%	0.3%
Education and Research	11.5%	12.7%	15.2%
Culture, Church and Recreation	0.2%	0.8%	0.9%
Transport and Communication	31.6%	32.5%	31.3%
Building industry and Real estate	3.7%	2.9%	3.2%
Electricity, gas, water and heating	1.9%	2.0%	1.9%
Justice	6.0%	6.3%	10.7%
Defence [1]	11.1%	11.0%	11.0%
Other purposes	12.5%	12.2%	10.7%
Local and County council government	867 200	951 900	1 134 100
In percentages: Management of the public sector	5.1%	4.8%	6.3%
Social welfare	31.5%	32.7%	34.1%
Health	40.3%	40.8%	31.5%
Education and Research	10.0%	9.2%	16.6%
Culture, Church and Recreation	6.1%	5.7%	4.5%
Transport and Communication	0.6%	0.5%	0.2%
Building industry and Real estate	2.9%	2.6%	2.1%
Electricity, gas, water and heating	1.9%	1.6%	0.6%
Justice	0.0%	0.0%	0.0%
Defence	0.0%	0.0%	0.0%
Other purposes	1.6%	2.2%	4.2%
TOTAL GOVERNMENT SECTOR	1 294 500	1 375 00	1 529 100

1.   Excluding conscripts.
Source: ''Statistics Information Series AM'', Statistics Sweden.

SWITZERLAND

Table 1. **Personnel in federal departments**

(annual averages)

	1987	1991	1993
Gerichte/Courts	144	192	208
Parlamentsdienste/Federal Assembly	47	83	105
Bundeskanzlei/Federal Chancellery	245	266	285
Foreign Affairs	1 755	1 863	1 879
Interior	7 512	7 685	7 647
Justice and Police	1 363	1 813	1 960
Military	14 753	14 820	14 476
Finance	5 797	6 139	6 266
Public Economy	1 769	1 832	1 875
Transport, Communications and Energy	508	580	667
TOTAL	33 893	35 273	35 368

Source: Federal Office of Personnel (*Eidgenössisches Personalamt*).

TURKEY

Table 1. **Personnel by levels of government, 1993**

Central administration:[1]	1 641 544
Civil servants	*1 436 307*
Contracted personnel	*12 657*
Permanent workers	*120 118*
Temporary workers	*72 462*
Special provincial administration	8 251
Municipalities[2]	256 550
Public economic enterprises:[3]	577 835
Public employees	*24 285*
Contracted personnel	*232 816*
Permanent workers	*215 660*
Temporary workers	*105 074*
TOTAL	2 484 180

1. Personnel of establishments with general budgets, annexed budgets, autonomous budgets and budgetary funds are included. Personnel of the General Secretariat of the Presidency, the Grand National Assembly, and the military personnel and General commandership of the Gendarmerie are excluded.
2. Including the personnel of metropolitan municipalities, but not of village administrations.
3. Enterprises covered by the privatisation programme are excluded.
Source: State Personnel Presidency; Ministry of Finance; Ministry of the Interior.

UNITED KINGDOM

Introduction

The United Kingdom definitions of "general government" and "public sector" are fully compatible with the concepts of the System of National Accounts (SNA).

Table 1. **Employment in main government departments**[1]

(full-time equivalents, as at April each year)

	1980	1985	1992	1993
Ministry of Agriculture, Fisheries and Food	13 800	11 400	9 800	10 000
Customs and Excise	27 200	25 400	26 400	25 100
Ministry of Defence[2]	218 000	174 100	139 500	129 200
Department of Employment[3]	50 700	54 700	57 100	57 400
Department of the Environment	48 300	32 800	20 700	15 000
Home Office[4]	34 100	36 600	49 700	51 400
Inland Revenue	78 300	69 800	68 900	66 500
Land Registry	5 900	6 800	9 600	9 200
Lord Chancellor's Department	10 000	10 200	11 600	11 900
Department of Social Security[5]	96 200	92 800	78 300	84 800
Department of Trade and Industry	7 200	12 600	11 400	11 800
Department of Transport	13 500	14 400	15 000	14 400
Other	101 700	57 400	67 400	67 400
TOTAL	704 900	599 000	565 300	554 200

1. Excluding Northern Ireland.
2. Excluding Royal Ordnance Factories.
3. Including the Advisory, Conciliation and Arbitration Service and the Health and Safety Executive.
4. Including Her Majesty's Prison Service.
5. Figures for the Department of Health and Social Security in 1980 and 1985.
Source: Her Majesty's Treasury.

Table 2. **Breakdown of civil servants in agencies and departments**[1]

(full-time equivalents)

	April 1992		October 1993	
	Numbers	Percentage	Numbers	Percentage
Agencies[2]	288 000	51	337 000	62
Announced agency candidates	69 000	12	23 000	4
Agency candidates under consideration	92 000	16	67 000	12
Remaining in departments	116 000	21	119 000	22
TOTAL CIVIL SERVICE	565 000	100	546 000	100

1. Excluding Northern Ireland.
2. Including departments operating fully on "Next Steps" lines.
Source: Office of Public Service and Science.

Table 3. **Public sector employment**

(full-time equivalents, mid-year figures)

	1980	1985	1992	1993
Central government:	2 196 000	2 144 000	1 823 000	1 481 000
Civil service	*700 000*	*596 000*	*567 000*	*551 000*
National Health Service	*1 001 000*	*1 030 000*	*750 000*	*438 000*
Armed forces	*323 000*	*326 000*	*290 000*	*271 000*
Other	*172 000*	*192 000*	*216 000*	*221 000*
Local government:	2 343 000	2 325 000	2 257 000	2 105 000
Education	*1 087 000*	*1 021 000*	*970 000*	*838 000*
Social service	*235 000*	*256 000*	*285 000*	*279 000*
Construction	*146 000*	*125 000*	*97 000*	*90 000*
Police	*176 000*	*182 000*	*199 000*	*201 000*
Other	*699 000*	*741 000*	*706 000*	*697 000*
TOTAL GENERAL GOVERNMENT	4 539 000	4 469 000	4 080 000	3 586 000
Public corporations:	2 007 000	1 236 000	810 000	1 030 000
Nationalised industries	*1 785 000*	*1 118 000*	*465 000*	*439 000*
Other	*222 000*	*118 000*	*345 000*	*591 000*
TOTAL PUBLIC SECTOR	6 546 000	5 705 000	4 890 000	4 616 000

Source: Economic Trends, January 1994, Central Statistical Office, Her Majesty's Treasury.

UNITED STATES

Introduction

Tables 1 to 3 are based on two sources, the U.S. Government and the Bureau of the Census, which nevertheless seem to have a very similar coverage. However, the U.S. Government source now includes military personnel on active duty from the regular armed forces (Department of Defense), from the Coast Guard (Department of Transportation) and from reserve forces. Excluded are non-active duty reserve forces. Also excluded are several tens of thousands of U.S. nationals working on a contract basis at federal government owned facilities (including military installations), such as research laboratories and manufacturing plants, and U.S. nationals working overseas.

A new table (Table 4) has been added which is taken from the monthly labour surveys by the Department of Labor. This source uses the Standard Industrial Classification 1987 (SIC) which contains the concept of public administration but also aggregates data into a government sector concept.

Table 1. **Employment in executive departments**

	September 1980	September 1985	January 1992	1993 (average)
Agriculture	129 139	117 750	113 496	114 600
Commerce [1]	48 563	35 150	37 563	36 100
Defense	960 116	1 084 549	1 006 120	960 200
Education	7 364	4 889	5 037	4 900
Energy	21 557	16 749	20 157	20 300
Health and Human Services	155 662	140 151	130 532	129 000
Housing and Urban Development	16 964	12 289	14 247	13 300
Interior	77 357	77 485	75 584	76 700
Justice	56 327	64 433	93 213	95 400
Labor	23 400	18 260	17 942	19 600
State	23 497	25 254	25 798	25 600
Transportation	72 361	62 227	70 131	69 900
Treasury	124 663	130 084	170 368	161 100
Veterans Affairs [2]	228 285	247 156	255 448	234 400
TOTAL	1 945 255	2 036 426	2 035 636	1 961 100

1.   Commerce employment expands significantly in decennial census years (1980).
2.   Veterans Affairs was not a Cabinet Department in 1980 nor 1985.
Source: U.S. Government.

Table 2.   **Employment in the federal government**

	September 1980	September 1985	January 1992	September 1993
Executive branch:	2 820 978	2 963 542	3 025 971	2 903 030
Executive Office of the President	*1 886*	*1 526*	*1 803*	*1 768*
Executive departments	*1 716 970*	*1 789 270*	*2 035 636*	*1 961 100*
Independent agencies[1]	*435 122*	*428 746*	*988 532*	*149 822*
Postal service	*667 000*	*744 000*	–	*790 340*
Legislative branch	39 710	38 764	38 696	38 258
Judicial branch	15 178	18 225	26 407	28 120
TOTAL CIVILIAN EMPLOYMENT	2 875 866	3 020 531	3 091 074	3 012 839
Active duty military personnel:	2 091 381	2 189 555	–	1 744 337
Department of Defense	*2 052 000*	*2 151 000*	–	*1 705 103*
Coast Guard (Department of Transportation)	*39 381*	*38 595*	–	*39 234*
TOTAL	4 967 247	5 410 126	3 091 074	4 757 176

– Data not available.
1.   Including Postal Service in 1992.
Source: U.S. Government.

Table 3.   **Civilian employment by level of government**

(number of persons, full-time and part-time)

	1980	1985	1990	1991
Federal government	2 898 000	3 021 000	3 105 000	3 103 000
State governments	3 753 000	3 984 000	4 503 000	4 521 000
Local governments:	9 562 000	9 685 000	10 762 000	10 930 000
Counties	*1 853 000*	*1 891 000*	*2 167 000*	*2 196 000*
Cities	*2 561 000*	*2 467 000*	*2 642 000*	*2 662 000*
Townships	*394 000*	*392 000*	*418 000*	*415 000*
School districts	*4 270 000*	*4 416 000*	*4 950 000*	*5 045 000*
Special districts	*484 000*	*519 000*	*585 000*	*612 000*
TOTAL	16 213 000	16 690 000	18 370 000	18 554 000

Source: Public Employment Series GE, Bureau of the Census.

Table 4.   **Civilian employment by industrial branch and institutional sector**

(november each year, in thousands)

	1980	1985	1990
FEDERAL GOVERNMENT	2 776.0	2 884.0	2 949.0
Executive branch	2 722.7	2 827.2	2 888.4
In percentages: Department of Defense	*33.0%*	*35.0%*	*32.0%*
U.S. Postal Service	*24.0%*	*27.0%*	*28.0%*
Other executive	*43.0%*	*38.0%*	*40.0%*
Legislative branch	38.7	38.5	37.3
Judicial branch	14.9	18.0	23.5
STATE GOVERNMENT	3 727.0	3 978.0	4 448.0
In percentages: State government hospitals	*14.0%*	*11.0%*	*10.0%*
State government education	*41.0%*	*42.0%*	*42.0%*
General administration[1]	*28.0%*	*32.0%*	*37.0%*
LOCAL GOVERNMENT	9 954.0	9 988.0	11 317.0
In percentages: Transportation and public utilities	*6.0%*	*5.0%*	*4.0%*
Local government hospitals	*6.0%*	*6.0%*	*6.0%*
Local government education	*55.0%*	*57.0%*	*57.0%*
General administration[1]	*29.0%*	*29.0%*	*30.0%*
TOTAL GOVERNMENT	16 457.0	16 850.0	18 714.0

1.   Including executive, legislative and judicial functions.
Source: Employment, Hours and Earning 1909-90, Vol. II, March 1991, U.S. Department of Labor.

Annex 2

LIST OF NATIONAL CORRESPONDENTS

Australia

Mr. W.J. BLICK
First Assistant Secretary
Government Division
Department of the Prime Minister and Cabinet
3-5 National Circuit
Canberra, A.C.T. 2600

Austria

Mrs. Lieselotte RICHTER
Head of Division IV/7
Federal Chancellery
Ballhausplatz 2
A-1014 Vienna

Belgium

M. Jean-Marie MOTTOUL
Chef de corps des Conseillers
de la fonction publique
Service d'administration générale
Ministère de l'Intérieur
et de la Fonction publique
19, boulevard Páchéco, Bte. 2
B-1010 Bruxelles

Canada

Ms. Yvette ALOÏSI
Officer/Agent
Machinery of Government Secretariat
Privy Council Office
Langevin Block, Room 312
Ottawa, Ontario K1A 0A3

Denmark

Mr. Jasper Steen WINKEL
Head of Section
Ministry of Finance
Christiansborg Slotsplads 1
DK-1218 Copenhagen K

Finland

Mr. Markku KIVINIEMI
Research Manager
Administrative Development Agency
P.L. 101
SF-00331 Helsinki

France

Mme Marie-Hélène POINSSOT
Sous Directeur de la modernisation et de la qualité
Direction générale de l'administration et de la
fonction publique
Ministère de la Fonction publique
32, rue de Babylone
F-75700 Paris

Germany

Dr. Dietmar SEILER
Director
Federal Academy of Public Administration
Friedrich-Ebert-Strasse 1
D-53173 Bonn (Bad Godesberg)

Greece

Mr. Vassilios ANDRONOPOULOS
Director-General
Ministry to the Presidency of Government
15, Vassilissis Sofias Avenue
GR-106 74 Athens

Iceland

Mr. Jón Ragnar BLÖNDAL
Head of Division
Ministry of Finance
Arnarhvoll
IS-150 Reykjavik

Ireland

Mr. Patrick J. MOORE
Assistant Secretary
Department of Finance
Agriculture House
Kildare Street
Dublin 2

Italy

Dr. Antonino VINCI
Directeur géneral
Département de la fonction publique
Présidence du Conseil des ministres
Palazzo Vidoni
Corso Vittorio Emanuele, 116
I-00186 Rome

Japan

Mr. Yukio YASUMURA
First Secretary
Japanese Delegation to the OECD
11, avenue Hoche
F-75008 Paris France

Luxembourg

M. Pierre NEYENS
Directeur de l'Administration
du personnel de l'État
Ministère de la Fonction publique
Bâtiment ''Le Royal-Arsenal''
12-14, avenue Émile Reuter
L-2420 Luxembourg

Netherlands

Ms. Veronique FRINKING
Department of the Secretary-General
Ministry of Home Affairs
Postbus 20011
NL-2500 EA The Hague

New Zealand

Mr. Don HUNN
State Services Commissioner
State Services Commission
100 Molesworth Street
P.O. Box 329
Wellington

Norway

Ms. Eva HILDRUM
Assistant Director General
Ministry of Government Administration
Postboks 8004 DEP.
N-0030 Oslo 1

Portugal

Mme Joana ORVALHO
Directeur
Secrétariat à la Modernisation administrative
Rua Almeida Brandão, 7-2°
P-1200 Lisbonne

Spain

M. Emilio CASALS PERALTA
Conseiller pour les affaires internationales
Ministère pour les Administrations publiques
Paseo de la Castellana, 3
E-28046 Madrid

Sweden

Mr. Bo RIDDARSTRÖM
Under-Secretary for Public Administration
Ministry of Finance
Drottninggatan 21
S-103 33 Stockholm

Switzerland

M. François COUCHEPIN
Chancelier de la Confédération suisse
Chancellerie fédérale
CH-3003 Berne

Turkey

Mrs. Reyyan ÖDEMIS
Director
Foreign Relations Department
Prime Ministry
Basbakanlik Dis Iliskiler Baskanligi
Basbakanlik Ek Binasi
Mesrutiyet Cad. No. 24, Kat. 5 Kizilay,
06640 Ankara

United Kingdom

Mr. Don WOOD
Office of Public Service and Science
Cabinet Office
Horse Guards Road
London SW1P 3AL

United States

Mr. Franklin S. REEDER
Deputy Assistant Director for Veterans Affairs
and Personnel
Office of Management and Budget
Executive Office of the President
17th and Pennsylvania Avenue, N.W.
Washington, D.C. 20503

MAIN SALES OUTLETS OF OECD PUBLICATIONS
PRINCIPAUX POINTS DE VENTE DES PUBLICATIONS DE L'OCDE

ARGENTINA – ARGENTINE
Carlos Hirsch S.R.L.
Galería Güemes, Florida 165, 4° Piso
1333 Buenos Aires   Tel. (1) 331.1787 y 331.2391
Telefax: (1) 331.1787

AUSTRALIA – AUSTRALIE
D.A. Information Services
648 Whitehorse Road, P.O.B 163
Mitcham, Victoria 3132   Tel. (03) 873.4411
Telefax: (03) 873.5679

AUSTRIA – AUTRICHE
Gerold & Co.
Graben 31
Wien I   Tel. (0222) 533.50.14

BELGIUM – BELGIQUE
Jean De Lannoy
Avenue du Roi 202
B-1060 Bruxelles   Tel. (02) 538.51.69/538.08.41
Telefax: (02) 538.08.41

CANADA
Renouf Publishing Company Ltd.
1294 Algoma Road
Ottawa, ON K1B 3W8   Tel. (613) 741.4333
Telefax: (613) 741.5439
Stores:
61 Sparks Street
Ottawa, ON K1P 5R1   Tel. (613) 238.8985
211 Yonge Street
Toronto, ON M5B 1M4   Tel. (416) 363.3171
Telefax: (416)363.59.63

Les Éditions La Liberté Inc.
3020 Chemin Sainte-Foy
Sainte-Foy, PQ G1X 3V6   Tel. (418) 658.3763
Telefax: (418) 658.3763

Federal Publications Inc.
165 University Avenue, Suite 701
Toronto, ON M5H 3B8   Tel. (416) 860.1611
Telefax: (416) 860.1608

Les Publications Fédérales
1185 Université
Montréal, QC H3B 3A7   Tel. (514) 954.1633
Telefax : (514) 954.1635

CHINA – CHINE
China National Publications Import
Export Corporation (CNPIEC)
16 Gongti E. Road, Chaoyang District
P.O. Box 88 or 50
Beijing 100704 PR   Tel. (01) 506.6688
Telefax: (01) 506.3101

DENMARK – DANEMARK
Munksgaard Book and Subscription Service
35, Nørre Søgade, P.O. Box 2148
DK-1016 København K   Tel. (33) 12.85.70
Telefax: (33) 12.93.87

FINLAND – FINLANDE
Akateeminen Kirjakauppa
Keskuskatu 1, P.O. Box 128
00100 Helsinki

Subscription Services/Agence d'abonnements :
P.O. Box 23
00371 Helsinki   Tel. (358 0) 12141
Telefax: (358 0) 121.4450

FRANCE
OECD/OCDE
Mail Orders/Commandes par correspondance:
2, rue André-Pascal
75775 Paris Cedex 16   Tel. (33-1) 45.24.82.00
Telefax: (33-1) 49.10.42.76
Telex: 640048 OCDE

OECD Bookshop/Librairie de l'OCDE :
33, rue Octave-Feuillet
75016 Paris   Tel. (33-1) 45.24.81.67
(33-1) 45.24.81.81
Documentation Française
29, quai Voltaire
75007 Paris   Tel. 40.15.70.00
Gibert Jeune (Droit-Économie)
6, place Saint-Michel
75006 Paris   Tel. 43.25.91.19
Librairie du Commerce International
10, avenue d'Iéna
75016 Paris   Tel. 40.73.34.60
Librairie Dunod
Université Paris-Dauphine
Place du Maréchal de Lattre de Tassigny
75016 Paris   Tel. (1) 44.05.40.13
Librairie Lavoisier
11, rue Lavoisier
75008 Paris   Tel. 42.65.39.95
Librairie L.G.D.J. - Montchrestien
20, rue Soufflot
75005 Paris   Tel. 46.33.89.85
Librairie des Sciences Politiques
30, rue Saint-Guillaume
75007 Paris   Tel. 45.48.36.02
P.U.F.
49, boulevard Saint-Michel
75005 Paris   Tel. 43.25.83.40
Librairie de l'Université
12a, rue Nazareth
13100 Aix-en-Provence   Tel. (16) 42.26.18.08
Documentation Française
165, rue Garibaldi
69003 Lyon   Tel. (16) 78.63.32.23
Librairie Decitre
29, place Bellecour
69002 Lyon   Tel. (16) 72.40.54.54

GERMANY – ALLEMAGNE
OECD Publications and Information Centre
August-Bebel-Allee 6
D-53175 Bonn   Tel. (0228) 959.120
Telefax: (0228) 959.12.17

GREECE – GRÈCE
Librairie Kauffmann
Mavrokordatou 9
106 78 Athens   Tel. (01) 32.55.321
Telefax: (01) 36.33.967

HONG-KONG
Swindon Book Co. Ltd.
13–15 Lock Road
Kowloon, Hong Kong   Tel. 366.80.31
Telefax: 739.49.75

HUNGARY – HONGRIE
Euro Info Service
Margitsziget, Európa Ház
1138 Budapest   Tel. (1) 111.62.16
Telefax : (1) 111.60.61

ICELAND – ISLANDE
Mál Mog Menning
Laugavegi 18, Pósthólf 392
121 Reykjavik   Tel. 162.35.23

INDIA – INDE
Oxford Book and Stationery Co.
Scindia House
New Delhi 110001   Tel.(11) 331.5896/5308
Telefax: (11) 332.5993
17 Park Street
Calcutta 700016   Tel. 240832

INDONESIA – INDONÉSIE
Pdii-Lipi
P.O. Box 269/JKSMG/88
Jakarta 12790   Tel. 583467
Telex: 62 875

ISRAEL
Praedicta
5 Shatner Street
P.O. Box 34030
Jerusalem 91430   Tel. (2) 52.84.90/1/2
Telefax: (2) 52.84.93
R.O.Y.
P.O. Box 13056
Tel Aviv 61130   Tél. (3) 49.61.08
Telefax (3) 544.60.39

ITALY – ITALIE
Libreria Commissionaria Sansoni
Via Duca di Calabria 1/1
50125 Firenze   Tel. (055) 64.54.15
Telefax: (055) 64.12.57
Via Bartolini 29
20155 Milano   Tel. (02) 36.50.83
Editrice e Libreria Herder
Piazza Montecitorio 120
00186 Roma   Tel. 679.46.28
Telefax: 678.47.51
Libreria Hoepli
Via Hoepli 5
20121 Milano   Tel. (02) 86.54.46
Telefax: (02) 805.28.86
Libreria Scientifica
Dott. Lucio de Biasio 'Aeiou'
Via Coronelli, 6
20146 Milano   Tel. (02) 48.95.45.52
Telefax: (02) 48.95.45.48

JAPAN – JAPON
OECD Publications and Information Centre
Landic Akasaka Building
2-3-4 Akasaka, Minato-ku
Tokyo 107   Tel. (81.3) 3586.2016
Telefax: (81.3) 3584.7929

KOREA – CORÉE
Kyobo Book Centre Co. Ltd.
P.O. Box 1658, Kwang Hwa Moon
Seoul   Tel. 730.78.91
Telefax: 735.00.30

MALAYSIA – MALAISIE
Co-operative Bookshop Ltd.
University of Malaya
P.O. Box 1127, Jalan Pantai Baru
59700 Kuala Lumpur
Malaysia   Tel. 756.5000/756.5425
Telefax: 757.3661

MEXICO – MEXIQUE
Revistas y Periodicos Internacionales S.A. de C.V.
Florencia 57 - 1004
Mexico, D.F. 06600   Tel. 207.81.00
Telefax : 208.39.79

NETHERLANDS – PAYS-BAS
SDU Uitgeverij Plantijnstraat
Externe Fondsen
Postbus 20014
2500 EA's-Gravenhage   Tel. (070) 37.89.880
Voor bestellingen: Telefax: (070) 34.75.778

NEW ZEALAND
NOUVELLE-ZÉLANDE
Legislation Services
P.O. Box 12418
Thorndon, Wellington   Tel. (04) 496.5652
Telefax: (04) 496.5698

NORWAY – NORVÈGE

Narvesen Info Center – NIC
Bertrand Narvesens vei 2
P.O. Box 6125 Etterstad
0602 Oslo 6 Tel. (022) 57.33.00
Telefax: (022) 68.19.01

PAKISTAN

Mirza Book Agency
65 Shahrah Quaid-E-Azam
Lahore 54000 Tel. (42) 353.601
Telefax: (42) 231.730

PHILIPPINE – PHILIPPINES

International Book Center
5th Floor, Filipinas Life Bldg.
Ayala Avenue
Metro Manila Tel. 81.96.76
Telex 23312 RHP PH

PORTUGAL

Livraria Portugal
Rua do Carmo 70-74
Apart. 2681
1200 Lisboa Tel.: (01) 347.49.82/5
Telefax: (01) 347.02.64

SINGAPORE – SINGAPOUR

Gower Asia Pacific Pte Ltd.
Golden Wheel Building
41, Kallang Pudding Road, No. 04-03
Singapore 1334 Tel. 741.5166
Telefax: 742.9356

SPAIN – ESPAGNE

Mundi-Prensa Libros S.A.
Castelló 37, Apartado 1223
Madrid 28001 Tel. (91) 431.33.99
Telefax: (91) 575.39.98

Libreria Internacional AEDOS
Consejo de Ciento 391
08009 – Barcelona Tel. (93) 488.30.09
Telefax: (93) 487.76.59
Llibreria de la Generalitat
Palau Moja
Rambla dels Estudis, 118
08002 – Barcelona
(Subscripcions) Tel. (93) 318.80.12
(Publicacions) Tel. (93) 302.67.23
Telefax: (93) 412.18.54

SRI LANKA

Centre for Policy Research
c/o Colombo Agencies Ltd.
No. 300-304, Galle Road
Colombo 3 Tel. (1) 574240, 573551-2
Telefax: (1) 575394, 510711

SWEDEN – SUÈDE

Fritzes Information Center
Box 16356
Regeringsgatan 12
106 47 Stockholm Tel. (08) 690.90.90
Telefax: (08) 20.50.21

Subscription Agency/Agence d'abonnements :
Wennergren-Williams Info AB
P.O. Box 1305
171 25 Solna Tel. (08) 705.97.50
Téléfax : (08) 27.00.71

SWITZERLAND – SUISSE

Maditec S.A. (Books and Periodicals - Livres
et périodiques)
Chemin des Palettes 4
Case postale 266
1020 Renens Tel. (021) 635.08.65
Telefax: (021) 635.07.80

Librairie Payot S.A.
4, place Pépinet
CP 3212
1002 Lausanne Tel. (021) 341.33.48
Telefax: (021) 341.33.45

Librairie Unilivres
6, rue de Candolle
1205 Genève Tel. (022) 320.26.23
Telefax: (022) 329.73.18

Subscription Agency/Agence d'abonnements :
Dynapresse Marketing S.A.
38 avenue Vibert
1227 Carouge Tel.: (022) 308.07.89
Telefax : (022) 308.07.99

See also – Voir aussi :
OECD Publications and Information Centre
August-Bebel-Allee 6
D-53175 Bonn (Germany) Tel. (0228) 959.120
Telefax: (0228) 959.12.17

TAIWAN – FORMOSE

Good Faith Worldwide Int'l. Co. Ltd.
9th Floor, No. 118, Sec. 2
Chung Hsiao E. Road
Taipei Tel. (02) 391.7396/391.7397
Telefax: (02) 394.9176

THAILAND – THAÏLANDE

Suksit Siam Co. Ltd.
113, 115 Fuang Nakhon Rd.
Opp. Wat Rajbopith
Bangkok 10200 Tel. (662) 225.9531/2
Telefax: (662) 222.5188

TURKEY – TURQUIE

Kültür Yayinlari Is-Türk Ltd. Sti.
Atatürk Bulvari No. 191/Kat 13
Kavaklidere/Ankara Tel. 428.11.40 Ext. 2458
Dolmabahce Cad. No. 29
Besiktas/Istanbul Tel. 260.71.88
Telex: 43482B

UNITED KINGDOM – ROYAUME-UNI

HMSO
Gen. enquiries Tel. (071) 873 0011
Postal orders only:
P.O. Box 276, London SW8 5DT
Personal Callers HMSO Bookshop
49 High Holborn, London WC1V 6HB
Telefax: (071) 873 8200
Branches at: Belfast, Birmingham, Bristol, Edin-
burgh, Manchester

UNITED STATES – ÉTATS-UNIS

OECD Publications and Information Centre
2001 L Street N.W., Suite 700
Washington, D.C. 20036-4910 Tel. (202) 785.6323
Telefax: (202) 785.0350

VENEZUELA

Libreria del Este
Avda F. Miranda 52, Aptdo. 60337
Edificio Galipán
Caracas 106 Tel. 951.1705/951.2307/951.1297
Telegram: Libreste Caracas

Subscription to OECD periodicals may also be placed through main subscription agencies.

Les abonnements aux publications périodiques de l'OCDE peuvent être souscrits auprès des principales agences d'abonnement.

Orders and inquiries from countries where Distributors have not yet been appointed should be sent to: OECD Publications Service, 2 rue André-Pascal, 75775 Paris Cedex 16, France.

Les commandes provenant de pays où l'OCDE n'a pas encore désigné de distributeur devraient être adressées à : OCDE, Service des Publications, 2, rue André-Pascal, 75775 Paris Cedex 16, France.

9-1994

OECD PUBLICATIONS, 2 rue André-Pascal, 75775 PARIS CEDEX 16
PRINTED IN FRANCE
(42 94 03 1) ISBN 92-64-14244-4 - No. 47447 1994